The Donkey's Ears

DOUGLAS DUNN

The Donkey's Ears

Politovsky's Letters Home

faber and faber

First published in Great Britain in 2000
By Faber and Faber Limited
3 Queen Square London WC1N 3AU

Typeset by Faber and Faber
Printed in England by MPG Books Ltd,
Victoria Square, Bodmin, Cornwall

A CIP record for this book
is available from the British Library

ISBN 0–571–20426–0

10 9 8 7 6 5 4 3 2 1

For Robbie and Lillias Dunn

also for
Lesley Bathgate
Frances Mullan
Kay Redfield Jamison
Liz Ogilvie and Bob Callender

and
IN MEMORIAM
E. S. Politovsky and
Sophie Politovsky

Acknowledgements

Part 1 of the poem was published in *Encounter* (November, 1983). Other excerpts appeared in *The Dark House* and *London Magazine*.

As ever, I'm grateful to the secretaries of The School of English and the St Andrews Scottish Studies Institute at the University of St Andrews for 'protecting my time' and other support during an over-long stint as Head of School and Director of the St Andrews Scottish Studies Institute. They are Dorothy Black, Frances Mullan, Jane Sommerville and Jill Gamble, and they are the best secretaries in the world. I'm also grateful to Elizabeth Pescod at the Literary and Philosophical Society of Newcastle for the loan of books, and to my friend the fine poet George Charlton for arranging these loans for me. I thank also the staff of the University Library at St Andrews for putting up with me.

The Donkey's Ears

Letters from Flag-Engineer E. S. Politovsky to his wife, written on board the flagship *Kniaz Suvorov*, 1904–1905, and based on the book *From Libau to Tsushima* (1906)

I

Tar-sticky bumboats chugged the anchorage
Among the bunting and rehearsing bands,
White hankies waved goodbye from women's hands
As caught deserters wailed in the dockyard cage.

Admiral Rozhestvensky's many ships
Steamed out of Kronstadt led by *Suvorov*.
A kettle trembled on the wardroom stove
Hot with the foretaste of apocalypse.

The Emperor, in the imperial yacht,
Sailed round his gun-saluting battle-fleet.
Salvoes of deference, loud, but obsolete
Gunnery, hailed our cap-waving despot.

Reval at dawn. That blank Courlandian shore!
Its miles of marram thrust a nothing on
My mind already numb with premonition
Cued by autumnal coastline metaphor.

An apopleptic captain came undone
In the serious regatta. Red-faced as ham
He turned his *Asia* into a ram
For the *Apraksin* in the rising sun.

II

It's half a season since you heard from me.
First, summer overlapped on autumn, now

It's wintry whistles on the flagship's prow
As hints of tundra chill our Russian sea.

But blue, my love. Our bearded priests serve mass
Shaking their Holy Water on the guns.
A Christian Navy! I noticed their ikons
Reflect a saint's eyes on our polished brass.

Tonight was dangerous and tense. We drowsed
With our boots on, the gun crews at their posts
Between the Danish and the Swedish coasts
And their civilian lights. Our searchlights browsed

Each indecisive swell, until, at dawn,
Grey European light revealed the fleet
Behind us, looking powerful, massive, neat –
Think of what taxes made this proud sea-brawn!

Today I have a rammed ship to repair –
Work, work. Our empire links two continents,
The Hermitage to Asiatic tents,
And I do service for its 'mighty Tsar'.

III

I pulled my sea-boots on, my mackintosh.
They're useless in this filth, this dirty wet.
My lubber peasantry get on with it,
Sea-sick and clumsy as their hammers crash.

My junior officers are just as bad,
Half-trained, work-shy, and puking as each dip
And rise contorts their guts, the rolling ship
A leaking, battered, worthless ironclad.

I ruined my trousers in the *Buistry*'s hold;
Its bilge-muds seeped above my knee-length boots
On treacled waves that lapped their liquid soots
With flakes of rust and paint and Viking cold.

We should have worked on deck, but the same sea
That keeps me from the *Suvorov*, rolled in
And swept the *Buistry*'s decks with northern brine.
Discomfort is the stuff of history!

I'll lie on the *Kamchatka*'s wardroom couch
Tonight, and write to you about our ships.
Think of me, Sophie, and dream you taste my lips.
Even at this stage, dried salt defines my touch.

IV

At lunch the admiral conferred on me
The Order of St Anne. He's aide-de-camp
To Nicholas and pandemonium.
No Pushkin for our Tsarist odyssey!

A ship's no city; it's a street in Hell.
I toured our sea- and self-inflicted scars,
Our leaks and damages. Black-faced stokers
Peeped from the portholes of their stinking fo'c'sle.

Black sudsy water by the bucketful
Sluiced down the runnels where the stokers washed.
On deck a careless saboteur was lashed.
Carbolic foam lapped at the Harveyed steel

As *Oryol*'s drums tapped to the punishment.
But blue, my dear, on this imperial sea

Where malcontents square with autocracy
That lays its judgement on skins of dissent.

V

We've wound our watches back. Britannic time
Inched on this cruising of the hemisphere
Reverses me by five knots back, my dear,
To you, to comfort and indoor sublime.

English, *Self-Taught* lies open and unread.
It's been a day of sweat and damaged boats.
'War news' goes round in rumoured anecdotes –
Misleading gossip mouthed by the misled.

I've been dozing, remembering yesterday
Lunching among the maps. Our Admiral's
Cigar smoke settled on its lazy whorls;
His map-room's sky dulled with Havana grey,

Clouding the global charts, while, like a ghost,
His spectral steward wiped the cognac stains
Ringed in wet liquor on the numbered mains,
Indelible off the Korean coast,

All eighteen thousand miles of buts and ifs
Away. His hand slid past – starched, spotless cuff! –
Mopping the sea-miles in the *Suvorov*,
Wiping the brandied bays and ash-flecked reefs.

VI

Lulled by moonlight: like warm autumn, it was,
Deep on the grassy plains, or watching stars

From windows looking out on city squares
When poplars rustle and the cafés close.

These airing stokers long for solid ground,
Cursing conscription and geography.
Heart-breaking moonlight bleaches on the sea.
A Russian navy takes the long way round.

Three thousand tons a day – they shovel coal
Down in their hot and grunting odium
And sing to moonlight with a lyric from
Old Russia's anachronistic soul.

A clockhand searchlight drops its silver on
Small waves that shatter it. From *Suvorov*
I watch these little lights float, thinking of
Your bird-crumbs scattered on a frosted lawn.

VII

All Europe claims a Scythian wanderlust
Impels our fleet towards the yellow East,
A sea-hoofed modern Mongolian beast
Armada'd in the Tsardom's permafrost.

Our enemy is everything that floats.
I stood on the afterbridge, hot from below,
And watched the needle searchlights stitch and sew
A fantasy of eight torpedo boats.

Guns flashed and sucked the air from ears and lungs,
Each white blink showing us how we might die
In nightmare, up-to-date mortality.
I left the bridge, rung by vibrating rung,

And from the afterdeck, I saw our lights
Rake up an empty smack, then hesitate
On gear and tackle, a civilian net,
As sitting targets in our gunners' sights.

Even a half-Lieutenant whom I've seen
Read treasonable pamphlets in his bunk
Went mad with bloodlust on the Dogger Bank
Prepared to die serving a six-inch gun.

If I'd been diligent with *English*, *Self-Taught*,
I might have had a name to put in this;
But it went down in white analysis
In the illiterate but polyglot

Atrocity of sea, blood on its deck
As up its stern heaved. Its legal light
Shone deep as garnets set against the night,
Red, red for 'Stop', that helpless rhetoric.

Our 'modern' fleet, iron arithmetic,
Metallurgy and engineering law,
Go down in scandal. A man beside me saw
Two fishermen hold up four half-dead haddock.

VIII

Aurora's holed below her waterline –
Imaginary, midnight Japanese!
Our guns were real, but not our enemies . . .
An empire, at its zenith, in decline!

In a gun-silence, the black *Suvorov*
Steams for the East, with priests and holy relics

While half the crew carries a crucifix,
Though it's a chaplain's had his hands blown off!

But now the wardroom dogs chase champagne corks
Across the floor, and bits of card on string.
Our midshipmen are remanoeuvring
Last night's 'attack' with sugar cubes and forks.

Pale stewards from the wardroom stoves serve tea
While officers of guns boast of the rate
Their magazines served shells up to them at,
Their ears cocked to obsessive gunnery.

I sit in a corner, my love, my glass
A perfect image of a small, clear sea.
Old hands at this game, we sit quietly,
And toast ourselves in vodka's veritas.

IX

So far, so far to sail. And then, for what?
I think it is the century compels us.
An antique nineteenth century expels us
And time's the mystery in which we're caught,

The web of 'progress' (meaning bigger guns).
And me, a poet! Sophie, be delighted
I work to hope I'll hear myself recited
After my labours on these damaged tons.

PART TWO

I

Fog-bound, unpeopled, legendary cliffs
Encourage Fillipovsky to confuse
King Lear with *Hamlet*. A literary cruise
For taffrail fops in rakish neckerchiefs!

Fresh from their *café-cognac* in the mess
They're sharing Fillipovsky's telescope
With doltish misquotations! Untidy rope
Provokes his wrath. He'd lash a man for less

Than idle seamanship – 'Under arrest!'
So much for him, an expert senior hand
Punished by an irrational command
Lisped by the under-read and overdressed.

Three hours from London; but, from over there,
Four hours by train to Paris! Smell the broth
Delivered to the gunners, the stink of cloth
Rained on and slept in . . . Freezing sailors swear

At the English morning. Gold *messaline*
De soie was your adored Parisian gown
Last year – you wore it with that hand-me-down
Samarkand shawl (ancestral plunder!), green,

Islamic green, oasis-coloured, adored
By everyone and loved by me, my dear.
Those white cliffs send signals of naval fear.
So early, but a man's jumped overboard,

Gone off his rocker in the narrow seas.
Captain Ignatzius taps the wardroom clock –
'Time and a life of miles to Vladivostok!'
The Channel grumbles, weary with increase.

II

Three dogs in the wardroom. Von Kürsel rants,
'Who's shaved this pup' – Flagmansky – 'for the tropics?'
Staff officers are canine disputants
Standing their ground on doggy politics.

One claims a chaplain did, but he denies it.
Such are our pastimes in this toxic ark.
He trained a dog, then tried to tyrannize it.
Now he shouts 'NO! NO!' in a pious bark.

III

Hamburg-Amerika's coal-laden tramps
Heave-to alongside, hull to buffered hull,
Our hireling colliers with their bunkers full.
A messman sells me Spanish postage stamps,

Crafty for profit, but illiterate.
Unnecessary officers relax
With a haircut, shoes raised to the bootblack's
Duster, its soothingly civilian pat.

'Good as a turn ashore,' Ignatzius says,
Posing a polished shoe. Leontiev's mad –
The barber soused him with the wrong pomade.
On deck, the creak and swing of the Temperleys.

Four officers they've blamed for firing on
Innocent trawlers on the Dogger Bank
Go off to walk the diplomatic plank –
Scapegoats our admiral hangs his bungling on.

But Rozhestvensky, too, 's packed Klado off,
That self-conceited bore and 'strategist',
Know-nothing self-styled expert, bad hand at whist,
Taking his pedantry and nasty cough.

The water-sprinting swans on Vigo Bay
Go where they go, into an anywhere
Sheltered for them, pair by domestic pair.
In nature there's no nationality.

IV

Nocturnal clearings and Hispanic stars,
The asterisks of God, an opulent
Notation of the sky, as in Tashkent –
Remember? – when, like paired astronomers

We saw the stars of Allah shine on us
And kissed and heard erotic harness bells
Affirm two honeymooning infidels –
Welcoming, Arabic, euphonious.

The things I noticed then and do not now,
Or can't, or notice now but didn't then –
South and disabled off the coast of Spain,
A Russian Sinbad in his armoured dhow!

Autumn-near-winter, in 1904,
My year of atlases come true, a year

Since Kazakhstan. I close down on Tangier,
Corsair and Barbary, its Moorish shore,

And I sense you, Sophie, and hold your hand
In a dreamt aroma as the Prophet's roar
Growls on the October surf, a metaphor
Describing Africa to Samarkand.

V

Haunted by British cruisers, *Oryol* collapsed
Around the strain of its unanswering wires,
Jamming its steering-gear. Nelsonian squires
Laughed as they watched our seamanship eclipsed

By their nimble patterns, our lumbering fleet
Black and lemon-yellow to their lean, warlike
Athletic grey, ruthless as Caspian pike,
Trafalgared, thorough, turning their sea-neat

Figures around us. Rozhestvensky cursed
Reservists for their landlocked innocence.
Men tremble in the forethought of such omens
Of ocean-war in which they're unrehearsed

Especially as they know their Admiral's
No genius when it comes to battle-tactics
Though very good at Romanov tyrannics,
And seeing right in wrong, and true in false.

VI

Ten years of Nicholas! Hurrah! Hurrah!
His anniversary on *Suvorov*

Cheers up our loyalty's official love,
Logged thus, as 'off the coast of Africa'.

Vodka below-decks and champagne above
As officers and drunken ratings share
Our servile State's conservative despair
Nursed on the regal lap of Romanov.

Cheers from the deck of sister *Borodino*
Draw our attention from imperial lunch.
Ignatzius chews, and, coughing on his munch,
He says, 'Pray for Napoleonic snow.'

VII

A lemon wind blew from the citrus groves
Before light rain. It's a great event
To a domestic man, this whiff of scent
From the planet's Moroccan alcoves.

Tonight I'm slave to my imagination.
All day I calculated, sketched, and dug
In Napier's tables in a dialogue
With facts and answers. Mathematician

To battleships, repairer of their faults,
I hate the sea's wrinkled mechanics, its
Full force of weathered sames and opposites
Rearing its only element, its salts

Ground in its seabed quarries. All night long
Our bands played as the men competed for
Prizes for fastest coaling, each competitor
A muscled serf to roubles and to song.

I sent a wire, Sophie, but no answer yet
Tapped over the blue Europe between us.
Telegraphed Morse-code's waltz-time's blurt and buzz
Finds me queued for you. Some get, most don't get

Telegraphed billets-doux, but scribbled joy
Sometimes, in the telegraphist's panache
As he decodes each cryptic dot and dash,
Shoves up his specs, and shouts it – 'It's a boy!'

PART THREE

I

A hot salt-water bath – ooh, ah – sea-suds
Curdled in brine, easing me out of work
In my half-candled cranny of the ark.
My servant mops bathwater from the bulkheads,

Condensation of me, my grey radiance
Dispersed in drips and then wrung from a rag
By deferential Golovko, a windbag
Who calls me 'sire', not 'sir', and makes me wince.

Dead calm tonight, closing on Senegal.
'Where's that?' my servant asks. He doesn't know!
I leaf the atlas. 'There,' I point, and show
The line of Cancer three days' sluggish trawl

Behind our sterns, and 'There!' I point, Dakar,
French Africa. 'Why are the Frenchmen there?'
His lumpy snout sniffs at a guessed-at answer.
The European Powers love afar,

Places not rightly theirs except by force.
Our empire, I explain, is continental,
Europe's and Asia's coincidental
Continuous geography. 'The horse,'

I tell him, 'is our natural ship of war.
But here we are, a navy sailing east
Around the world to beat the yellow beast
Who's shelling the hell out of our Port Arthur.'

'Where's Vladivostok, sire?' My finger draws
An oceanic sweat-trail on the page.
Like God, I halt our smoky pilgrimage
At havens uttered with a finger's pause.

Wherever he comes from, he isn't daft.
He smiles, and I know what he means, his eye
Somewhere between a patriotic cry
For who he is and hate for where. He laughed.

II

Coal everywhere on deck, in passageways,
Sacks in the cabins and a liquid dust
Baked on our bodies like a racial crust,
Sunbeamed beneath the fans like negligées

On absent women, a momentary cool
Fleshpot of you, Sophie. Black beggars tout
For kopecks off each ironclad redoubt –
A spray of coins, then the unbeautiful

Servile display of diving, small change, trade
For Gambia souvenirs, each iced glass nursed
As medicine against incessant thirst,
But coal-dust floating on the lemonade.

I took my turn ashore, hoping to drink
A long, well-iced, refreshing glass of beer
Somewhere alone, and think of you, my dear.
I wanted to be earthed with time to think.

Instead I found my baby engineers
Rancidly drunk among the native whores –

A Russian embrace on tropic shores! –
My Yuris, Nikolais and Vladimirs.

We buried Nelidov who died of heat.
'Sunstroke,' the doctor said. 'Sickbays are full.
Our lousy Admiral's one of God's old school
To make men work in such a sun! Conceit,

'I call it. Naval tyranny. We ought
To tell him so.' Poor Nelidov could speak
Eight languages, but died in a unique
Delirium – his cough was polyglot.

I had my French beer and, indeed, drank three!
A very decent, very French café.
Then went to see poor Nelidov away,
Wishing him alive, or buried at sea,

That professional sailor, truly up-to-date
At what we do, and what we'll have to do
When we arrive at war, and our rendezvous
Wherever at an armoured tête-à-tête.

III

Beheaded, then they soak them in a pond
Until they marinade to succulence
In cannibal Gabon's primordial fens.
Civilization's decidedly postponed

By three millennia and a meat shortage.
Two Europeans guzzled in a month! –
Kidnapped and gourmet'd down a labyrinth
Called native lunch. A belch of human pottage.

We visited the king of this lush spot –
At seventy-two, he's recently enthroned –
Imagining his chef with cleavers honed
And martyred Jesuits stewing in his pot.

His sag-dugged dowagers begged for Russian coins.
A hammocked queen slugged equatorial rum.
Grassed like a haystack, to a tum-tum-tum,
A dancer cast the witchcraft of his loins.

Edenic botany, my love, high palms,
Mimosa, and, lonely at night, I feel
Nocturnal perfumes, aromatic steel,
Waft on the water over fragrant rhythms.

Trinkets and toys – no place to spend your days,
This Libreville, where the fruit-eating French
Hear Paris and its traffic in a conch,
Backwatered French colonial emigrés.

IV

Golovko hadn't heard of it before –
The slave trade. 'Slav means slave? I didn't know . . .'
He likes to learn and feel his knowledge grow,
Although he reads and writes. I should deplore

His ignorance, but can't. I sympathize.
We ought to teach our people how to read.
Instead, we keep it to ourselves, and plead
That pacts with progress never can be wise.

Oryol's appalling skipper's dumped overboard
His entire ship's library, on the grounds

That he'd already made it out of bounds
To crewmen who could read because it 'poured

'Oil on political fire', making sure
Sedition, mutiny, and insubordination.
Pushkin, Tolstoy, Chekhov, all were thrown in –
Atlantic waves of Russian literature!

But Slavs like us, named for the haltered slaves
Antiquity demanded, need to hate
Miasmic suffering, the pathetic weight
History heaps here in exported graves

To the Americas. But how we live
Depends on servants, service, servitude.
The Slav, the African, the multitude . . .
Our truths are difficult and elusive.

Golovko gasped, but I could see him thinking
Hard on identity and how he loathes
Ignorance on him like ill-fitting clothes.
I poured out vodka, and, while we were drinking,

I told him more of Africa, the slave trade,
And did more of the atlas, showing him
Where we were going, and, literatim,
Names of places, an exotic parade,

A big fanfare of names. Such names! Such places!
So far from home, you learn what made you choose
The sea and difference, the mermaid Muse
Who casts her spells across the wind-swept spaces

Between the there and there, and whose uncharted
Distances no one yet has understood.

With care, by latitude and longitude,
You go there, but you find she's just departed

For somewhere else, another temptress name
Thousands of miles across the lovely globe
Which she invites your broken heart to probe –
But all you'll see 's the flicker, not the flame.

Golovko loves it when I speak like this.
'My God, sire, but I'd no idea blacks . . .
Slaves, Slavs, like us? By God, sire, us kulaks
Should kick ourselves for sheer know-nothingness. . .'

v

Sea-holy rituals, crossing the Equator,
Neptune with trident and a flaxen beard,
A boy got up as Venus, brassièred
Boy-goddess, and the Symbolic Navigator . . .

Men watched the drama from the foreturret,
Perched on the crosstrees, on the yards and masts
In an exploded pyramid of castes –
An admiral, his officers, a water-butt

For democratic ducking, and no one saved
From the misrule, high-jinks and carnival.
'Good,' Ignatzius said. 'Good for men's morale' –
Facing an outsized razor, duly shaved.

Free for a day, each man a mutineer
Beyond the reach of law or etiquette
Other than Neptune's. Everyman gets wet
When crossing to the southern hemisphere.

Fictitious secrecy. Pamphlets and tracts
Discovered in the sweaty fo'c'sles prove
Rebellious limits to political love.
Crazed with the joyful mischief of our *Pax*

Equatoria, we could forget the seethe
Below-decks where the hidden policemen skulk
In every unofficial prison-hulk,
This fleet of fools, this dangerous air we breathe.

VI

It is a dream of thought, milk of the wind
As white as poetry, an innocent
Dreamt in the being of its own event
Off Great Fish Bay, a priestly, abstract mind.

Proconsul of the stormy southern sea,
It is the ghost of us, this albatross
Over *Malay*, an emblematic loss
Alone in South Atlantic history.

An albatross, an eye's thought, loping wingspan,
Lonely, imperious, its potent flight
Soared through my dreams most of a troubled night.
How far we've sailed on this cruise to Japan!

Decks crack and groan; the bulkheads squeak and strain
In the falling temperature. Doors shut again,
Shrinking. Wood eases back and drawers open.
South-westerlies afflict the weather-vane.

Our Hanseatic merchantmen bring coal
From Cardiff and a cold wind delivers

Degrees that chill us worse than Baltic's shivers.
Thinking of snow and ice revives my soul.

Sophie, my work is hard. My expertise
Demands too much of me. My engineers
Lack skill before the furious hydrosphere's
Energies. They're waiting, those Japanese.

VII

I can't describe the sea. For who am I
To say an element? At Lüderitz
Palatial waves crashed on the forward turrets.
Salt through my pores, salt-water in my eye

En route to the *Kamchatka* in the storm –
Not night, not weather, that insomniac
Substance, piled high and huge, a molten black
Amazement to the principles of warm

And comfort, but pure ocean in a mood
Devoted to slow anger and against
Inhibited, controlled, and too-much-fenced
Forms of the world, or active solitude

Conducted with vigour, eternal noise
And movement, heave, waves high as hills forcing
Gut-sink and gut-rise, faint-headed cursing
From men who when they stepped aboard were boys.

Call it eternal merely, call it fact,
Or element, but call it Ocean first,
For if you don't then voyages are cursed.
To go to sea like this means you transact

With powers beyond the force of ships and guns,
Armour and engineering, steel, and men,
But with recurrent fates, again, and again,
No matter numbers, honours, guns, or tons.

The sea's lore has it that an albatross
Means a departed skipper's lonely soul.
Old hands believe that sad and wonderful
Story. I smile and watch the bird. Pathos,

Indeed, but it's because it mates for life.
One bird alone means widower or widow,
Or one unmatched yet, feathered belle or beau –
Anyway, lacking a husband or wife.

VIII

So, Portuguese Angola, German South-
West Africa, the Belgian Congo, and the French,
The British Empire, Spanish . . . Inch by inch,
They colonize the globe, and mouth by mouth

The peoples of the world learn how to speak
In languages their mothers didn't sing –
The continental woe, the suffering,
The strong, the weak, the mighty, and the meek.

IX

It's an amazing sight to see a big fleet
Before the mercies of a vivid sea,
And that means damage, therefore work for me.
Our men are new, our ships are obsolete,

Officers stupid, and our men, though brave,
Show signs of discontent. The Ocean nods,
Heaves, storms, as if it is a thing of God's.
It is. It's elemental, and a grave.

St Nicholas' Day! Off the Cape of Good Hope!
Tzarskoe Selo, Petersburg, Kronstadt,
Tashkent, but here's a different habitat,
One not prefigured in the horoscope

You had that gypsy cast for me last year –
So much for her astrology! And yet,
The stars I've seen, such stars, make me regret
My lack of superstition, my austere

Reason and science. Ignatzius says I'm dull.
'You've no poetic soul. You calculate
Too much, my dear. You *ratiocinate*.
You state, but can't imagine. A holed hull

'Excites you more than Lermontov or Pushkin.
But I suppose we need your kind,' he sighed,
Theatrically, as if he almost died
To think someone like me should underpin

His far more glamorous notions of the sea.
He doesn't know that there's a poet aboard,
Albeit one of whom he's never heard,
And that this secret versifier's me!

The crew plays silly deck-games, getting wet.
Mass, prayers, and a salute. My telescope
Showed me the famous, shapeless face of 'Good Hope',
A landmark I'm unlikely to forget

Among the many others seen, and those to come.
We'll leave the South Atlantic soon and steam
Through the Indian Ocean. It's like a dream.
Today we're at our furthest point from home.

A ship's been following us, like Nemesis.
We've known this many times. Astronomers
Like us, though, can ignore foreigners,
Probably British, snooping, relentless,

For we're observed by stars, and study stars.
Mesmerized by heavens, by the stellar,
It is as if we find out who we are,
Bemused and lonely at our escritoires.

X

Huge swells, troughs measured seventy feet deep . . .
The sight of big ships vanishing is such
I can't describe it. I can only clutch
At my heart when the miraculous upsweep

Delivers them. And thus we go, rising
And sinking, rising. Wet through all day long,
All night on *Suvorov*, the sea too strong,
Too wild, too evil, utterly surprising

For me to get to ships with damaged gear
Or engines. I've been signalling advice,
Which doesn't get there. It's a throw of dice.
We're at the mercy of God's gondolier

On this demented Ocean. I don't pray,
As you know. Bold Ignatzius does! His knees,

Poetic knees, are scabbed with kneeling. 'Please!
Please!' Give me rational science any day,

None of this holy nonsense, holding forth
For respite from a storm. I'll pray in this
Communion with you, Sophie, each versed kiss
In my reports to you a thing of worth.

Love makes the world go round. I know. I go
Around the world, and you go with me, day
By day. What's left for me to say, but say
I see you in the smoke from my tobacco,

Your shape in a wraith-image everywhere
Perking me up, making me glad, not sad,
Your dutiful and engineering nomad
Devoted to repairing disrepair.

Kamchatka signalled that her coal was bad.
We'd seen her black reek as she dropped astern
In the Indian Ocean's curious swell and churn –
Kamchatka, workshop for our Iliad

When we 'get there'. She asked to dump her coal
But Rozhestvensky said, 'Throw overboard
Your saboteur, your master of discord.
Look for a disaffected Finn or Pole.'

But nearing Sainte Marie, off Madagascar,
We've heard the dismal news, the Eastern Fleet
Sunk by the Japanese, a big defeat.
They're saying prayers – the fools! – for the Tsar.

Say prayers, I say, for friends of mine, and yours,
Sophie, gone down, perhaps, outside Port Arthur,

While we steam now round northern Madagascar,
Grievous, watching the stars, and the future's

Uncertainty, essential unknowingness.
We are much disheartened, and very depressed.
I browse my lips on your remembered breasts.
I solve myself on an imagined kiss.

PART FOUR

I

Farewell's perfectionists, but here we are
Arriving somewhere else, trying to look
Flag-proud, unbattered, trim, and storybook.
No bigger fleet's been seen off Madagascar!

'A voyage like this,' Ignatzius said, 'would be
Worth more than all this trouble if we found
A serious chunk of undiscovered ground
Instead of a French jail. This Sainte Marie,

''s a Devil's Island annex, a convict colony
For dissident or criminal natives,
But here we are, in our Muscovian sieves,
Presented with a perfect irony –

'Anchored alongside tropical Siberia!
Mon cher, I find this very hard. You see,
– And keep this secret – I'm drawn to "liberty".
I've had enough of Admiralty blah,

'Corruption, bribes, stupidity, mistakes.
Poetic soul should find its purpose in
People, not Field-Marshal Kuropatkin
Inert in Mukden with parades and wakes

'For friends in Port Arthur.' We've heard the news.
Port Arthur's fallen. Forty thousand men!
The First Pacific Fleet, the garrison,
Gone down before the Japanese . . .

What a disaster! Rozhestvensky prowled
Around the dismal news, pacing the bridge,
Old, overdressed, starched, searching for courage
Or words sincere enough, or not befouled

By rhetoric, that might say what he felt.
'We must avenge the First Pacific Fleet.
Our honour is to snatch from their defeat
A victory that turns around the insult

'To our Empire and its Tsar. God save the Tsar!'
A very general cheer. I was amazed
To hear disaster's culprit cheered and praised,
And then again, 'Hurrah! Hurrah! Hurrah!'

A lousy rhetoric goes down a treat.
Say 'vengeance' and the common man gets angry.
It doesn't matter if he's tired and hungry.
Throw him an enemy, and it's a sweet

And simplified salvation from his cares,
The way I was with Jews, and though my guilt
Goes deep enough, anti-Semitic silt
Clogging my brain and active thoroughfares

Of temperament and mind with prejudice,
It doesn't make much sense to blame our news
On fifteen thousand emigrated Jews
In Cape Town, dodging military service,

Or so men say, although we've Jews on board
Serving no worse than others for a State
Protected by manipulative hate,
Cossacks, evictions, pogroms, servile fraud.

Ignatzius's sobbing cynicism slid
Into a tantrum in which Jews were blamed.
I half-agreed with him. Now, though, ashamed
Beside a private lamp, low-spirited,

I know the blame lies with our kind, our caste,
Our hopeless leadership, dyed-in-the-wool
Autocracy, corruption and misrule.
A 'saboteur' swings from the mizzenmast.

II

December 19th, but it's New Year's Day
On the New Style calendar. I went ashore
And gathered pretty shells, a good five score.
My souvenirs increase and they'll portray

My voyage for you. I've a native bow,
With arrows, a spear, a shield, a sculpted 'god',
Six curious and sinister masks, an odd
Necklace of beaten copper, a chapeau

Fashioned from straw and parrot feathers, some
Mysterious trinkets and a vicious club
Carved with the markings of Beelzebub,
Ditto my prized cannibals' tom-tom drum.

Pet-loving Fillipovsky bought a snake,
A little python which, with any luck,
Will grow, and one night choke the whining cluck
Out of his foppish throat. I bellyache

When I'm alone, talking to myself, my nib
Toxic with pent-up loathing for that sort,

These boastful princelings, good for balls at Court.
On active service, though, the cut of their jib

Reeks of anachronism. Potentates!
High on bravado, low on common sense,
They're 'well connected', but intelligence
They somehow failed to contact. Inebriates,

Mess-specialists, workshy wardroom diehards,
With their pet monkeys and parrots, fawning
Before the Admiral, *boeuf Bourguignon*-ing
From their own special chef, with bodyguards

From the Marines each time they step on deck –
Don't ask me to approve, because I won't.
You see, I haven't changed! I'm still as blunt,
Still your familiar and old-fashioned stiffneck

Engineer, and in love with modern things,
Not antique protocol or good Court manners,
But boilers, machines, and common spanners.
Problems, solutions – these are my blessings.

Lieutenant Korkorovsky's self-regard
Annoyed me. I'd have had him on a charge
Were self-conceit a crime. Even as large
As his is, the bloated, wealthy blowhard

Thrives in immunity, though he's a dud.
But Rozhestvensky dotes on his 'young men',
His *corps d'élite*. I do the work of ten
While they adorn us with their 'noble' blood.

Admiral Folkerzham's fleet they say 's arrived
By way of Suez and at Nossi-Bé.

I'm tired, my darling. I'm filled with dismay.
I've worked so hard while these suave others skived.

III

A stoker died on board the *Oslyabya*.
She fired her guns and gave his body up
To the great sea. This moved me. I can put up
Even with half-masted colours, but there's a

Stranger mood around. I met the man once
On an inspection visit. He'd dug coal
In a Ukrainian mine. Such is the null
Mind of conscriptive bureaucracy, they pounce

On miners and turn them into stokers – coal,
You see. So *he* was 'well connected' too –
Coal. But he'd never seen the sea, the blue,
The grey of it, its affront to the soul

Of a landsman like him. I am so sad
To think of our good workers come to grief.
'Why five o'clock, when our *apéritif*
Lingers upon the tray? It's all too bad,

'This timing,' an officer lisped. 'You'd think
Old Rozhestvensky more considerate
Than have us all on deck at five, the shit,
Postponing our deserved first evening drink!'

'I heard that,' I said. 'Oh, I'm sorry, Flag.'
'Salute me when you speak to me, you dolt!
Stand to attention! Don't you dare insult
My dead companion. You, you drunken windbag,

'What've *you* done to get the Fleet this far?'
It doesn't do to lose your temper with
Noble riffraff. December twentieth,
Old Style! But what's a few days where we are?

I measure everything. Exactitude!
And I time this nocturnal barcarole
On each delivered rhyme, my whispered call
Across such weeks and miles and solitude.

IV

When a fleet rounds a Cape, turning a corner
Takes on a meaning different to the one
Familiar from streets – another sensation
Entirely. Or am I still a mourner

For that dead digger of coal and misled
By memories of '*Kol Slaven*', the dirge played
By several bands, a mournful accolade
Disjointed by the wind, the tune of the dead?

Turning a corner of geography
We've reached a calmer anchorage but learn
The Japanese might just be miles astern.
Time's made physical in Tang-tang Bay.

You turn a corner (as it were), but it's the same
Constantly replicated precipice
And sense of miles and time and endlessness,
Nothing fixed down, reliable, or tame,

Domestic, certain, somewhere one could love.
At battle stations, with torpedo nets

Spread rocking on the waves, ships' silhouettes
In tropical dusk-light, and *Suvorov*

Closed up for action, even the fops awake
And looking lively where they should be, time
Turns into cliché, standing still, sublime
And dangerous, and all for a mistake.

Perhaps the Japanese are near. But why
Leave home and base to fight a battle when
All that they need to do is wait and then
When we arrive put out to sea, fresh and spry?

I find this obvious, but the Admiral needs
Emergencies to keep crews on their toes.
Or so I tend to think, but no one knows
What Rozhestvensky thinks or how he reads

Those 'intercepted signals' – Japanese,
Apparently, but how could they be here
So soon after the fall of Port Arthur?
Like us, they're finite and with massive seas

Between us and them; but I admit it –
It would be fitting if we met half-way
In mid Indian Ocean, our navy
And their navy. Highly appropriate!

Not easy, though, to find each other on
This wonderful and inconvenient globe.
They'll know our whereabouts. The British probe,
Their masts cleverly just on the horizon.

Why take a risk, and send their fleet down here,
When they can stay in home waters, and wait

While we tire ourselves on this elaborate
Voyage, this epic exercise of gear,

Coal, steel, men, and not much thought, this fleet?
Our men are discontent, some criminals
Let loose from jail and told to serve, or else,
Others half-trained, unfit, and no élite.

I see so many of them, and I see
Much to admire in how some do their best.
I'm no revolutionary, but they're oppressed.
'Who, on a warship, though, calls himself "free"?'

I said to someone. He scratched his head and smiled.
'I wouldn't mind if I'd been "free" on shore,'
He said, grinning. 'I've been to sea before.
But this is war. I'd like to leave my child

'Something. Not much. The chance of not being me.
I'd put it that way, sir. Opportunity.
And not a life like mine, scarred with pity,
Departures, sorrows, and going to sea

'To earn a pittance that you can't send home.
Why, sir, are we forbidden to send our pay
Back to our families? The Admiralty?
Yes, a rule, but a bad one. It'll come

'To trouble, sir,' he whispered. 'Believe me, sir.
Most men are grieved. I'm not a mutineer
By nature, sir, for I'm an engineer,
Like you, and I'm no sneaky whisperer

'Either, but I can sense a head of steam
Below decks, and I'd say it's serious.'

I've kept this quiet. With whom could I discuss
This blow to Rozhestvensky's self-esteem?

V

I wonder what Christ thinks of Christendom,
Whose birth-date's different on two calendars?
The Magi wouldn't recognize those stars
Tonight, the celestial ad infinitum

Of southern regions still undiscovered
In His time. Our Russian Christmas 's come!
It would feel good to say, 'I'm going home!'
I don't look as I did – I've grown a beard.

Thirty-one-gun salutes all round and prayers
Then Rozhestvensky's speech, the best I've heard
Him give, each measured, understated word
Unlike his usual style – tyrannic airs

And graces, hectoring, blame made to stick
On anyone but him. The Dogger Bank –
He *still* insists that furious, futile prank
Of panic was a Japanese attack,

Torpedo boats using the fishing fleet
As cover. True enough, the Japanese
Order their vessels from the Tyne and Tees
And other British shipyards, but it cheats

Reason to think the British would permit
Our enemy the use of ports, and if
Albion's perfidiousness as water-bailiff
Is well known, then the Double-Eagle's wit

Ought not to stoop to Rozhestvensky's dim,
Obstinate refusal to admit that funk
Caused all that mayhem on the Dogger Bank.
So what can Christ think of his Christendom

Here on southern oceans, closed up for war
Against the Asiatic Japanese,
Destruction's armadas on the Seven Seas
Intent on victory, slaughter, and gore?

Not much.
            My beard doesn't itch, and it saves
Time, although it makes me look too 'Tsarist'.
Will you wonder what it feels like to be kissed
By me with a beard? But Golovko's 'shaves'

Began to frighten me. He's kind enough,
Polite enough, but feigns a brainlessness
Too easy to see through as artifice.
His cover's blown, and soon I'll call his bluff.

I wrote of corners earlier. Now I dream
Cornerless steppes, the multi-cornered forests,
The pure abstraction of these wooded mists
In the bee-forest, landlocked, interim.

VI

Unsounded waters and an imperfect chart
Reduce the fleet to sluggishness, one knot
In line ahead, the speed of soundsmen's thought,
Serving their navigators' prudent art.

Verse, too, is cautious, as it finds its way
Through depths and shallows, always looking for

Celestial heights above, the ocean floor
Below, the highs and lows of life, its play

With sorrows, joys and griefs, its ups and downs,
Its all-too-celebrated crests and troughs.
Enough of metaphor! That stuff's for toffs
Who went to school on it and who'd pronounce –

Ignatzius *would*! – my feeble verse too cautious,
Too much an engineer's spannered response
To everyday emotions and sensations
While short on the artistic and audacious.

Golovko found my jottings and *protested*.
'I served a master once. *He* was a scribbler.
His hair fell out! I warn your worship. Sir,
As well as bald, he got himself *arrested*!'

I swore the man to silence. We get on
Better than most paired officers and servants.
He neither touts, nor drops conspicuous hints,
Nor rifles through my cabin when I'm gone –

I'd left my notebook open, having been forced
To run to an emergency last night.
I wasn't *sure* that he can read and write –
And that last piece unfinished and half-versed! –

But now I know he can, because he said
(Can you believe it?) that his wife, too
(It startles me!) is Sophie! And it's true.
He showed a letter from her, and he read

It out – perfectly! – then signed off with her name.
We shook hands and embraced in tears for this

Coincidence and the name on a kiss.
Master and servant, whose wives' names are the same!

Later, called out to fix another ship,
I worried: Could good old Golovko be
A policeman and his supervision me?
Such times, that master-servant comradeship

Attracts suspicious thoughts! I feel ashamed
But wonder if that man who lost his hair
(If not fictitious) cursed his unaware
Embrace for two wives virtuously named.

Shallow seas continue, and, with dunting hulls,
Damage, repairs. – Our navigators are
Better at distance and a charted star
Than close-up, intimate, perfected skills.

Golovko with his letter, though – like mine,
It's old, from Libau . . . Men, reading old letters,
Servants, ratings, and their so-called 'betters',
There being no new ones for our paper shrines . . .

Handwriting on the eye is such a pleasure,
Sophie, that it's too hard to say why
A temperament of hand delights the eye,
Read, re-read, stared at, at our lonely leisure.

A different sort of speech from the Admiral's
Emotional calls to God, Country and War,
Russia, Destiny and the great Emperor!
I sit by this bug-beaded lamp and feel my pulse.

Mayhem aboard the *Roland* – mutiny!
Biedovy's ordered to arrest the lot
And Rozhestvensky fears a general plot
On hand, not knowing it's our destiny.

The night before, I finished my report
On the battleships, and didn't shirk the truth.
I'll make enemies. They'll call me a loudmouth,
'Not one of us', by no means 'a good sport'.

I mean to be useful, for Heaven's sake!
Poor naval architecture's not my fault –
I'm true to my profession and my salt
And not the sort of man to bellyache.

The mutineers submitted. It appears
Stokers rebelled against additional work
When two fell ill. The others went berserk.
They're practically civilians, not mutineers,

But Rozhestvensky's hot for punishment.
He threw a bottle at a midshipman
Just yesterday, and dreads the clandestine
Passing from hand to hand of radical print

In the furtive passageways of battleships
And cruisers, feeling sure – of course, he's right –
Conspirators in the below-decks' night
Discuss disaster and apocalypse.

He'd do far better if he'd turn his mind
To what ought to be done. Should we go on
Now that Port Arthur and its fleet have gone?
Or should we wait here, orderless, half-blind,

Informed by foreign newspapers, or go home?
He's not the sort to criticize the Tsar's
Advisers, other admirals, or Mars,
Stuck fast in an immovable syndrome

Devoted to obedience and a law
Insisting on honour, but still unaware
Modernity's made slaughter out of warfare
Whether on sea or land, explosive awe,

Statistics which someone like me knows far
Too much about.
                    Those mutineers were brave,
But wrong, or almost right. But who can save
Them now? Not Rozhestvensky. Not the Tsar.

Who can postpone or stop this merciless
Near-circumnavigation, this witless sprint
Over the oceans to the Orient,
To destiny?
                    Madame, I crave your kiss!

VIII

The bands were playing 'Little Russia'. Outside,
From my porthole, I saw a bay, calm sea,
Hills (some well-timbered). I felt myself free
For a moment, almost revivified.

So, this is Nossi-Bé. Our naval might
(What's left of it) now comes together here
On still waters. Folkerzham left Tangiers
For Suez and the relative delights

Good ports and harbours offer to a Fleet.
The Admirals embraced. So, here we are,
For God knows how long stuck off Madagascar,
Our strategy a matter of deceit,

Conceit, postponement, subterfuge, and worse.
We're strong, but inefficient. No one knows.
We all sit down, and ponder, and suppose.
God help us. We affront the universe.

Is it humanity, or is it us
Alone, refuses to face facts of war
In favour of a mediaeval 'honour'?
On both counts, Yes. There's nothing to discuss

On such questions. Strategy dictates ethics.
Nothing matters other than what's ordered
By our weary, over-epauletted warlord
Who sees the Ocean as his private Styx.

I know we'll wait here. I can feel the pause
Beginning in my blood as beat by beat
My blood slows and the engines of the Fleet
Run down beyond silence, the quiet laws

Machines obey. Instead, a stillness such
As no one other than an engineer
Can understand, someone like me, whose ear
Makes sense of sleeping boilers, warm to the touch

Now, cooling, and a muscled lethargy
In all that stillness, agitated sleep
And dust subsiding on each bunkered heap
Of Cardiff coal and shovelled energy.

PART FIVE

I

Seventy ships in one big basin sit.
Humidity's at 98 per cent.
What no one measures, though, 's the discontent,
Anxiety, the indeterminate

Muddle from which miasmic fear 's released.
You can't count spirit. Our bluejackets chafe
For vodka, women, home, and feeling safe
Somewhere utopian and unpoliced.

English seafarers call it Fiddler's Green,
A heaven of bottle, bed, and merriment.
Sailors can make mayhem benevolent,
Dear Sophie. It's as if all things marine

Demand excess. Because the life's so bold
And elemental on the dangerous sea,
Crowded, and lonely, ordered, and unfree,
As well as international, very old

In its traditions, our bluejackets claim
(But don't dare say so) that they want *their* share
Of Fiddler's Green, and that they should prepare,
Now, this minute, for posthumous fame.

They can't wait till they're dead! And I can't blame them.
They're lining up in queues for the jolly-boats
To take them off to sow their wild oats
In Helville. That's its name, a homonym

For hellraisers, although the pause I sense,
This stillness all around us, damp, and hot,
Creates a vision, not just of lust and tot,
But revolution and irreverence.

II

If nothing else, Helville's economy booms
On Russian gold. Prices shoot through the roof.
Asking a price, you'd better be shockproof
In Helville's squalid, overcrowded taprooms.

Whores are in short supply. Their ancient trade's
Transacted from a row of makeshift huts
Or in the bush. The Admiral tut-tuts.
In mercantile, colonial arcades

French, local and Pondicherry's profiteers
Fleece all and sundry. Suddenly, they're rich
Scratching a Russian navy's manic itch
For rotgut cognac and for Helville beer's

Improvement over shipboard water, itch
For women and a craving for good food,
An itch for momentary plenitude
And never mind the crooks it might enrich.

For what's the difference between pimps and Tsars
Who pack men off to fight on distant seas
And treat them badly as a lower species
And cheat them in imperial bazaars?

Forbidden to send wages home, what else
Will men do on an epic cruise like this

Other than spend them on the famished kiss
Vodka provides, or on temptation's impulse?

I don't blame them. The *Café Parisienne* –
It didn't have a name before – is where
Ignatzius and I (the debonair
Ignatzius!) sat down like drinking men

Intent on getting well and truly plastered,
Two gentlemen, not of Verona, but
Two thirsty gentlemen in a Helville hut.
You know me well enough. I'm not a drunkard.

Fond of a bottle, though (as you are too,
My dear), I rather think these stressful times
(Also these sultry, hot and humid climes)
Why I consumed more Madagascar Dew

Than I could hold. You know I never sing.
Well, I was singing, and Ignatzius sang –
Italian opera, the whole shebang!
We flew home, sideways, on a batwing.

III

The colibri is the world's smallest bird,
And I've seen one, so there. Also I've seen
The local cemetery – no Fiddler's Green,
I can asssure you. Among the graves I heard

Strange birdcalls and the cries of animals
All nameless to me. It was very weird,
Looking at graves while nameless creatures jeered.
This climate makes sickness in multiples.

Already some have sickness in their ears,
Some sort of fungoid growth, while others lapse
Strangely, and so soon, in this weathertrap's
Heat and humidity, the rain like tears

Wept by the ikons sent by the good ladies
Who run The Society to Help the Wounded,
Received today. But sickness is unbounded.
Doctors complain they lack the expertise

To treat exotic disease. They suggest
That melancholia's the reason why
So many men fall ill, decline, and die,
Lonely, moaning for home, and uncaressed.

Colibris aren't as small as I'd supposed
But small enough for me to sense their size
As very small, and therefore sympathize –
A bird, a battleship, the juxtaposed

Diminutive and mighty, tiny grace,
Then modern, manmade, armoured self-esteem.
Our planet's always bigger than it seems
Even from this highly imperfect place.

IV

Infinite birches in the frost and snow –
That was my dream last night. I can't think why
When I was born to worship Tashkent's sky,
Dry sun, and not this damp inferno.

Heat got to me in the Post Office queue.
Such is the climate, stamps are sold ungummed.

It's bad enough, with all five senses numbed,
Without a cadging search for paste or glue

To fix your stamps and send your letters home.
Predictably, Post Office clerks sold off
Their stocks of gum, and now a lousy toff
Next door in a grass kiosk – filthy gnome! –

Sells you a smear of it for two-francs-fifty.
That's more than postage costs! The men grow wild.
They feel themselves defrauded and defiled.
You'll know I paid up. I was never thrifty

But even so I find myself indignant
At how the French authorities conspire
With low-life traders. Who's in whose hire? –
I wonder. But they're just like us, asquint

For profitable opportunity,
Delinquent chance, corruption and the hope
Officialdom will leave them all the scope
They need to profit with impunity.

Blend in my dreaming of those frosted birches
With Romanov incompetence, the high hand
Taken with everything, you'll understand
Why I'm reluctant to believe the searches

My sleeping mind makes in instinctive truth.
It's just a stereotype, a picture from
Intuitive and much-loved, much-missed home
Gone wrong, or fudged, and leaving me a sleuth

Devoted to detection of my dreams,
Those fragile, frosted birches, and the snow

Witnessed as if through a prophetic window
Into a world of white, of hints, and screams.

V

Men look as if they've mined the coal they've piled
In holds and bunkers, stored in passageways.
Earth, air, fire and water! Technology's
Reshuffled elements are these four wild

Ingredients put to use in 1905's
Destructive warfare when a 12-inch shell
Could blow these sooty ruffians to Hell
In little pieces. Something old survives,

Though, in a modern Navy, 'hearts of oak',
As the English say. But how to Russianize it?
It might do better if we modernize it,
Face up to dysentery, sedition, sunstroke,

With realism, not a hankering for
Old Vitus Bering on the Bering Sea
And how he could inspire us – even me! –
With sacrificial legends of the war

Against distance, which is discovery's
Struggle with time and space. Imperial crawl
Over geography until you own it all
And pay for it in bankrupt treasuries –

That's why we're here, at war. We touched Japan's
Ambitions in Asia; theirs touched ours.
Who's fleets and armies have the greatest powers?
Who's got the cleverest military man?

It all depends on history and morale.
Looked at this way, we ought to turn and run,
Sail from the rising to the setting sun,
Or take the Trans-Siberian Canal!

VI

Picture the *Suvorov* alive with beasts
Among the heaps of coal. Oxen on deck
Wait for slaughter; through each black bottleneck
Hens, geese, and ducks behave like madcap guests

Among the monkeys and a porcupine.
I'm not the only one who's grown a beard.
Ignatzius says that mine looks 'engineered'
While his is Romanov or leonine.

He's still as dapper, even when drinking from
A jam-jar, all the wardroom's glassware smashed
In gales or mayhem, broken, swept, and trashed
From the Dogger Bank to Pandemonium.

Think of the litter that we've trailed behind us,
Our wash of ordure, swill and broken glass
Dumped into Ocean's infinite crevasse.
Its liquid mouths, its mobile jaws, remind us

Men, too, are dropped there. How could we forget?
Ignatzius says I'm morbid, but it's not
Morbidity that gives rise to the thought
More dead will join the dead on the swelling wet

Vast watermass. Nor is our Fleet alone
Among armadas which have trudged these seas.

The Spanish, English, Dutch, and Portuguese
Trailblazed into this hell-hole Francophone

Backwater of disaster and decline.
I'm not mad, Sophie. I'm certain of it.
In fact, I'd claim that I'm the opposite.
Today I ran into the 'mad Ensign'

On the *Malay*. At first I thought him sane,
But drunk, white-uniformed, bare-footed, capless,
A man who'd passed his morning on the piss
(Or days, maybe) enjoying the cool rain

On deck, the sobering hiss of rain on steel.
He took my hand and shook it. 'Sir, I know you!
I am Titov!' I thought, 'Who do I know, who,
Called Titov? No one! Does his beard conceal

'Someone I know?' He asked, 'Do you fear Death?
Have you seen him?' He paused, and the rain fell.
It dropped from waterlogged and tropic Hell.
They say they know you. That's the shibboleth

Lunatics establish. Then he laughed out loud,
Spreading his arms, and pointing, 'All this is
The armoured filth and spawn of Russia's
Mistakes, and *cruelty*, its floating shroud,

'Its sheer *incompetence* . . .' I thrust my hand
Against his mouth and gagged him. '*Romanov*'
Slipped through. I struggled. '*Shit*!' then '*hate*' then '*love*'
Pressed through my fingers – words tattoo'd on my hand.

Later, my work done, hot, and very tired,
Sweating (the rain stopped), I saw float past

Dead birds, dead beasts, and an iconoclast
Whose ideals failed to match those he desired.

VII

Rumours aboard a rumoured fleet make sense
But more gets through about Sebastopol
And mutiny. Rozhestvensky 'd keelhaul
Subversives, but it's French Intelligence

Whispers the news to Russian officers.
Communiqués from Rozhestvensky's bridge
Write wordless rhetoric, a verbiage,
A silent breeding ground for saboteurs.

We've crammed the sick, the drunkards, lunatics,
Prisoners, and men dismissed from service, on
Malay and concentrated dis- and un-,
Our negatives, our bads, our worses, sicks,

Aboard a single ship. They'll be sent home.
Or will be once its mutinous crew's been dealt with –
The *Malay*'s captain 's been threatened with death.
I dreamt last night that he'd been held to ransom,

The price for his release being *Malay*'s freedom.
Thus granted, *Malay* and her crew turned pirates
On the High Seas, among the Oceans' thickets,
Water's invisibilities and spacious welcome.

But I woke up, and Rozhestvensky too.
Marines surprised them. Drunk, or half-asleep,
The mutineers were rounded up like sheep
And *Malay*'s decks combed through and through and through

For 'evidence', as if they needed it,
Before the prompt trial on the *Suvorov*
Pressed on below the judgements of above –
Mere banishment, not firing squad or gibbet.

After a few days in battleship cells –
No ventilation, on water and bread,
In solitary, then if they're not dead
They're to be cast ashore, let loose on Hell's

Beaches. One miscreant blubbered, hoping for
Anything other than Madagascar's
Backwatered coastline, distant from the Tsar's
'Mercy' (he said), going over the score

In his frantic pleading. Strange, how subversives
Alter their causes after they've been caught
And plead for the forgiveness of the despot
They've conspired and struggled against. Motives!

Ah yes, motives! Virtue's momentum stops
When called to book by Admiralty law,
And empire, not just person, made of straw,
Salutes the million-saluted cap, then drops.

VIII

I overheard a crewman say those men
Condemned to being beached on Madagascar
Should kneel and pray and thank their lucky stars
They're spared the likely but still God-knows-when

Disaster Rozhestvensky has in mind
Guided by idiot deskbound strategists

Back home – Klado! – by paper tempests,
Inkwell battleplans, and speculative grind.

The mutineers could join the Foreign Legion,
A regiment of epauletted secrets.
Such name-changed scoundrels and unfortunates
Police the French possessions. Origin

Means nothing in the Legion's ranks, much feared
In Madagascar. Russians enlist
By the hundred, I'm told – the exiled fist,
Embittered bayonet and transferred fear.

Those prisoners, though – they feel that being 'marooned'
Means something lethal, and not an escape
From ships and a command less than shipshape,
Inexpert and improperly Neptuned.

True, half the officers are amateurs
And more than half the men out-elemented.
No wonder, then, so many are demented,
A soft touch for their fo'c'sle orators.

Few seem to notice, though, how many men
Have grown into their sea-legs and composure.
Instead of cursing and displeasure
Exaggerated in the name of discipline

We ought to recognize success, reward it,
Reform the nature of command, improve,
Not model what we do on Romanov
Autocracy, where officers lord it

And lower ranks put up with what's imposed.
Don't worry, dear. Anger, affront, and drink

Won't lead me to speak out what I might think.
I do my duty, keeping my mouth closed,

Lips sealed, etcetera. Please, rest assured
My revolutionary worries are
Directed at what's happening where *you* are,
Which I know little of, other than rumoured

Reports of riots, unrest, massacres.
Too much to ask, that our Admiralty keep
Its Fleet informed. They sacrifice our sleep,
Protecting the Tsar's, and his exchequer's.

IX

Torpor sets in, because the Admiral sleeps,
Or seems to. Only his *aide-de-camp*
Sees him these days, these days of tedium
On seventy anchored, sweltering scrapheaps.

The taste of coaldust in a cigarette,
Jampotted vodka, pestilential bugs,
Surly, rag-dressed sailors' insolent shrugs,
Monkeys, haggard parrots that shriek and fret,

While day by day demoralizing heat
Settles on languid card-games. Flaking paint.
Unpolished brass. Coal everywhere. The faint
But still pervasive stink of rotting meat.

All these, and more. Disorder's lethargy.
Half of our officers don't shift from bed
Unless to eat or drink, the leaders led
By animal appetites, their energy

Sweated from them, and their indiscipline
Infectious. Having caught it from the top
It drips, it seeps, and drop by tiny drop
Spreads everywhere from its first origin.

I *try* to keep busy. Despair's postponed;
It's not prevented. I, too, feel touched by
A loathesomely unanswerable *Why?* –
Slavonic, choral, mournful, baritoned

Out of the depths of forests. Drunken sorrow
Sings over the hot, ship-lit nocturnal bay,
Its rolling tune of grief a melody
In love with suffering and fated woe.

          X

I dreamt our rooms again. I think I haunt them.
I walk around and watch you read or sew.
Outside, the soft, cold cleanliness of snow,
A laundered paradise. But I don't want them,

These dreams, inevitable dreams of you.
Ten thousand men surviving on escape
Into their memories of a lover's shape,
A shadow cast by mind, a rendezvous

With home and trust! Our sleeping Admiral,
Does he, too, travel by the mind's moon-chart
Into the friendlier corners of his heart
Where truths and cares become conjectural?

Leontiev, staring at a photograph,
Felt I was there, and without looking up,

Said, sipping vodka from a broken cup,
'For all my foppishness, each hopeless gaffe

'I've stumbled through my life with, my mistakes,
I've loved, Flag, and been loved. If nothing else
I've known that frantic quickening of the pulse,
Proverbial pangs, and thunderclaps, and aches.'

And Fillipovsky, stretched on a wardroom sofa,
Studied gripped letters with tears in his eyes.
'If only, Flag, I hadn't told her lies.
I'm not a coward, but I *am* a loafer.

'Why don't they send our mail? For God's sake, why?
I need to know her answer!' Living in despair,
Men learn about themselves, and each nightmare
Discovery adds to an interior cry,

Self's silent scream; and *Suvorov* resounds
With cries and sighs, including mine, my dear.
The noise of self-recrimination, fear,
Absence, apartness, goes its dismal rounds

And even blithe Ignatzius 's withdrawn
Into his soul. In his case, it's a book
By Chekhov. He gave me such a look
Of sheer despair, contempt, and then a yawn

I'd never witnessed in my life before.
'*Ennui de fin de siècle*! I thought I'd done that!
God damn me, Flag, for an aristocrat,
A naval officer and dandy! Pour

'A tot, and one for me. What I must say
Might shock you. Should we take steps to replace

Our conked-out Admiral? I skipper this,
You know, his flagship. I'm his protégé,

'But he's asleep, or sick, and the Fleet rots
Without orders. The Admiralty won't
Advise me. They say "wait" or they say "don't".
They're in the grip of Klado's tricks and plots.

'And Folkerzham's not interested. Claims
It goes against all sorts of protocol.
Ask me, though, and I'd say that alcohol
Rules *his* roost *pro tem*, while he fears for blame's

'Stigma against his "reputation". Chekhov.
I met him once. Did I ever tell you?
No? . . . Rozhestvensky! What should we *do*?
We're all in Hell, my dear, wherein, whereof

'And hitherto, and notwithstanding, time,
Duty, business, and command, weigh heavily.
You know me, Flag. You know I can be silly.
It's my pretence. I'd love a more sublime

'Profession, but tradition chose, and here
I lounge before you with my Chekhov
Whose stories might explain us. But my love,
My love, believe me, is the Fleet, my fear

'That we might lose it. Friend, what should we *do*?'
All I could say was that we should do *something*.
He said he'd sleep on it. Yes, sleep's the thing
These days. Sleep, sleep, my love, until our rescue.

Awakened by official French complaints
That Helville's huts were being torn down by
His sailors, Rozhestvensky's angry cry
Stirred the entire Fleet, and roused the saints.

All of a sudden, Rozhestvensky quit
Cabin and bed and set about command.
All officers were roused from their divan'd,
Unsober heavens. Lucid, explicit

Orders of the Day were issued and signalled
Throughout the Fleet. – No shore leave's authorized,
All officers and men roundly chastised
As a disgrace to the Navy, unequalled

In all its 'long annals' of good service to
Our Tsars, all decks scrubbed, paint renewed,
Brass burnished, all shipshape, and good.
(I want my dream again, where I kiss you

In the no-time of unplaced night, not this
Manic remembrance of what's to be done
At the last minute.) I stood in the sun,
Hungover but relieved, and sent my kiss

Transmitted from a gun-glint straight to you
In a drum-and-bugled morning in Nossi-Bé
Where Rozhestvensky's new-found sanity
Cracked suddenly its *cock-a-doodle-do*!

Menageries tossed overboard, and drill,
Drill, drill, for all and sundry twice a day
And kit inspections now our holiday
From duty's over and the Admiral

Restored to health or sense or maybe both.
I led the flagship's stokers in PT.
Imagine, callisthenics, done by me,
Sophie, leading the others, me, a sloth

At physical jerks . . . I see the need for it
Although in shorts and singlet in such heat
Your lumbering engineer, this un-*petite*
Sample of manhood proved himself unfit!

How many cigarettes are smoked a day
Aboard the Russian Fleet? Who *doesn't* smoke?
Men fall down coughing. One – I fear heatstroke –
Dropped sweatless and was stretchered off to sickbay

While Rozhestvensky from the quarterdeck
Watched us, expressionless, and supervised
Artificers and stokers he surprised
With sheer command and his delayed henpeck

Discipline, forcing everyone to shift
Or face a firing-squad or punishment
Battalion in Siberia, a stint
In Sakhalin, or else be cast adrift

On Madagascar's exiled and remote
Distance from anywhere. It's distance, sheer
Far-offness, fills men with despair and fear,
Their ignorance of where they are. Untaught,

Half- or unlettered, *where* and *why* to them
Form questions they can't answer, unless told.
For information, they're left unconsoled –
Statistics in an autocratic system.

But jumping up and down, polishing brass,
Scrubbing the decks, at least on *Suvorov*,
They're put to work, while working their socks off
Suits the beliefs of those who sail First Class.

XIII

'Ringleaders' from the *Nakhimov* were shot
At dawn today, all fourteen – you, you, you,
Picked from a mutinous and half-starved crew
Guilty of hunger, and a counterplot

Rigged by their officers. The firing squad's
Admonitory echoes – fourteen times
Repeated by the rifles' mournful rhymes!
No wonder ratings think of us as frauds

When mutiny was hushed up first, and then
Because they'd dared protest a lack of bread
And Rozhestvensky feared complaints would spread,
Nakhimov's officers begged that their men

Face the full penalty. But it's well known
These self-indulgent swine, these overfed
Aristocrats, think nothing of mere bread
Or any staple that might lower their tone

While disobedience from the lower decks
Challenges power, champagne and caviare,

Romanov style, its ruthless repertoire,
Though what I see are Russian seabed wrecks.

Bad meat abounds. They toss it overboard
As dainties for the tyranny of sharks
Teeming around us, these iconic autarchs,
Ferocious, primitively self-assured.

XIV

Political discussions don't amuse me.
They're far too serious. Each faction loses
Part of its power, and history excuses
Excess and struggle, both of which confuse me

– Not one, not two, nor three, but several sides
Competing for the truth, and claiming it
While simultaneously maiming it.
These months have seen me learn much of the tides,

Less of the times, something of what men do
In unfamiliar circumstances, led
Incompetently and deprived of bread,
Though truths like these are marginally true,

Or don't add much when seen against events
You're living through back home, of which we're told
Too little, all our news of you controlled
By calculated dribbles and *per cents*.

XV

Rumours seep through. I don't know what to say.
After the stint of 'getting back to normal'

Boyarin Rozhestvensky ordered sea-drill
To make us fit to go to sea today.

Mirrors, and crockery (what's left of it)
Were stored, hatches closed down, and out we sailed.
We noticed that the Fleet was being tailed
By French torpedo-boats, champing at the bit

To catch us up (which wasn't hard to do).
Buistry peeled off to pick up telegrams
From the French, tricky even in these calms,
Suddenly rainless, tropical, and blue;

But neatly done, and well-observed by us,
Deckcrews attentive while their officers
Studied the business through binoculars
Or telescopes, wondering what messages

Required such speed for their delivery.
Buistry then brought them to the Admiral
On *Suvorov*, by rope and crane, less skill
Than bluffers' hope, I thought, a jittery

Transaction on a slow swell, heaving seas,
But calm for these waters. Then silence fell.
Two hours of an impatient, newsless Hell,
Then, after that, our orders, like a tease,

For gunnery rehearsals, 'throat clearing',
Work, work, work, most crews distracted from
Duty by troubles happening at home
And me and mine by hectic engineering.

Our shot fell nearer to the torpedo-boats
Than the canvas targets they were towing,

Much to their consternation. Some seagoing
Oared whalers tugging lines of tented targets

Capsized in the big spout of a near miss
While *Alexander III* and *Borodino*
Almost collided, why I'll never know.
Ten drowned, but otherwise disasterless –

A fair day's work for our under-rehearsed
Armada, learning – gunnery's neophytes –
How to use Barr and Stroud's latest gun-sights.
Is this the bad news, or could it be the worst? –

There's one instruction manual to go round
Suvorov, *Borodino*, and *Alexander*,
And that was 'lost' before flagged memoranda
Admitted, finally, that it was found –

Unopened, nor in Russian, I dare say.
An Order of the Day enlists all men
Who know the English tongue, and use a pen.
They're ordered to report to Rozhestvensky

In person. Can a late translation save
A Fleet from its incompetence? Men serve.
What's courage, though, when it's robbed of the nerve
Modernity provides, which will outbrave

Obsolete heroics, no matter the sheer
Valour presented to an enemy
Better equipped on the same shared sea,
Facing the same potential grave and fear?

English-trained Admiral Togo's Japanese
But English-built armadas scare me stiff.

Their Barr and Stroud sights pose no but-and-if
Translation to them, nor do ennui's

Aristocrats staff his Fleet.
                         Wardroom whispers.
We're ordered home. Or on to Vladivostok.
The rumoured soup tonight is manioc.
They haven't made their minds up. The chef stirs

Tropical porridge. 'Splash in vodka there!'
He shouts, grimacing at his wooden spoon.
'*Filet de singe* and *ragoût de baboun*,
But *à la russe*, a banquet for despair!'

XVI

What should we trust, our country or our luck?
It's sad to feel forgotten, waiting for mail
Remote from home and kiss at the taffrail
Under an awning rapidly rain-struck

As if inside a drum. Ignatzius speaks:
'What gets my goat is Admiralty scorn
Expressed through carelessness, all that highborn
Presumption that blue-blooded witless cliques

'Possess the right to tell us what to do
When none of them, not one, 's familiar with
Modernity, or knows the twentieth
Century's four years in. They haven't a clue!'

That from the captain of the *Suvorov*,
The flagship's skipper! Others look tight-lipped,
Suspicious, sensing a self-censorshipped
Personal silence might leave them better off

In police reports, nod sullenly and shrug,
Passing the cracked decanter. Others, though,
Grow thoughtful with experience, and each beau
And dandy's lost much of his scornful, smug,

Arrogant patriotism. Leontiev, say,
Kissed half his noble foppishness farewell
When rolled half-naked through the town of Hell,
Caked in the pissed-on mud of its Champs Elysées!

The other half departed when his ship
Came close to ramming *Alexander III*
The other day. An end to his ennui!
I read his mind through its self-censorship

And read von Kürsel's festering discontent,
His new-found sense of duty and his pride.
When men like these turn into dignified
Sea-officers, then I feel jubilant.

We're not so bad. We're learning on the keel
(Not on the hoof!). Or would be if our masters
Consulted experts, not astrologers,
Nor paper strategists, to prove our steel

Worthy of battle. But our Admiral,
Our Admiralty, drag indecisive heels.
Indecision's fidgets, their mind-wheels
Turn on their covert spokes, a rationale

Ignoring facts, the dangers that we face.
Neglected, who can feel surprised our crews
Discuss despair and wonder at the news
From home with indignation's rattled grace?

Grace, though. Believe me, I've detected it
In how men face the truths of loneliness,
Womanless, childless lives robbed of a kiss
And life made bearable with valiant wit.

XVII

Two thousand killed in Petersburg, it's rumoured,
And thousands wounded – just the sort of news
To brighten up this doltish, static cruise
And keep ten thousand restless men good humoured!

I think they lie. Could such a thing be fact?
Stuck here, in this warm rain, in this stiff heat,
This thick inertia, we're obsolete
Before we've even had a chance to act

On the tilting sea-stage we were chosen for,
Pushed to one side by Admiralty decisions
As if to prove the thickness of our skins,
Our tedious loyalty's *esprit de corps*.

I hadn't even noticed how my beard
Outgrew itself. Its shaggy, hirsute mass
Burgeoned and dangled, trying to surpass
Barbarian, unbarbered hair, the feared,

Face-filled, angry expression of morale
Gone all to pot. When men don't look in mirrors
Their looks impersonate instinctive terrors,
A primitive and fearful rationale.

Ignatzius and the Admiral complained.
'Inverted vanity, or reversed pride,'

Ignatzius said. 'I think your soul has died.
Time for a trim. We'll all be entertained

'Spectating Michael shear your whiskers back
To something like normality. Behave!
For you're the only engineer we have.'
So I consented. *Snick-snick snackety-snack*.

I didn't recognize myself! There was my face.
My private revolution! Scissored hair
Brought back identity from disrepair –
My feelings were elation and disgrace.

XVIII

I went aboard *Kiev* and *Vladimir*
Early this morning, but the air was hot.
Your trimmed, near-beardless, blear-eyed argonaut,
This fearless and intrepid engineer,

Stood in the prow, wearing his new pith helmet!
How's that for a transformation! Don't think
I'll give up eating meat, or give up drink –
I've steadied myself, but there's a limit.

Given the state of things, I was ordered –
Ignatzius's command – to go well armed.
I strapped the holster on and felt alarmed,
Pig-ignorant, civilian, and revolvered.

But these are happy ships. The *Vladimir*'s
Officers welcomed me with smiles and handshakes
Instead of diffidence and bellyaches.
Their crews and officers are *volunteers*,

And that's the secret of a competent,
Contented and well-ordered Navy, not
Conscripted peasants, men who never thought
They'd find themselves in this predicament,

For whom the sea was something that they'd heard of,
But never seen, or ever thought to choose,
Or if *invited* to, then they'd refuse.
But *asking* is beyond the Romanov.

You see how revolutionary I've become?
Although I worked hard, today was *courteous*,
No grumbling, no unnecessary fuss,
Just getting on with it, and then, when home

Cropped up in conversation over lunch –
Inevitably – I learned more about
What's happened. Their wardroom's less in doubt
Than ours – the flagship's! It's come to a crunch

Concerning information. *Vladimir*'s
Freer officers know more than we get told
By Rozhestvensky's mean, over-controlled
Release of news, as if the Admiral fears

Mutiny might stem from true disclosures.
He's shut himself away again. Confined
With ciphers and champagne, our mastermind
Investigates what a mere chart obscures,

The vast reality of many ships
Half-way to destiny, in need of coal,
Replenishments, morale, command, control,
And mastery darkened by mental eclipse.

XIX

What's this I do? A diary or a poem?
Or letters to you? Will you keep them by you
As a memento of my love, my blue
Seafaring days, and when you're old, read them

All over again, in your favourite chair
By the window? By then, much might have changed.
And how might Russia be rearranged
Forty years on? Mechanical corsair,

Maestro of naval architecture, algebraist,
Gifted in numbers and materials,
Devoted, though, to poetry, the skills
Of lines and engineering, unprejudiced

Before the arts and sciences, I hope for
Long life, to see modernity come true
In marriage and companionship with you.
In Nature, Sophie, there's no *either/or*

But history is all alternatives,
Decisions and mistakes, the right, the wrong,
The virtues of the weak, and of the strong.
It doesn't write itself; and it forgives

Nothing and no one in its chronicles
For lies and fudges in the end get told
And end up swinging from a printed scaffold.
The truth I'm pointing at 's old as the hills.

Although I want to, I might not survive
This armoured jaunt across too many seas.
I'm not being morbid. I'd just like you, please,
To know that if I don't come back alive,

Then you loved truly once, and could again.
Therefore, dear Sophie, I want you to trust
The future, not to treat it with disgust.
Mourn, if you must. But there are other men.

Don't get me wrong. I'm planning to come home.
But if I don't, then you should live your life
As you, not as my widow, or my wife.
But please, look after this, my only poem.

XX

I've put a brave face on these last few weeks.
Time, now, to tell the truth. Haircut and shave,
Radical laundry, won't help me outbrave –
They're far too superficial, these techniques –

Despair and apathy. Like others here,
I function through appearances; my mind,
Though, struggles with routines it once defined
As duty and knowledge. These were crystal-clear

Among my pieties. My mind is crushed.
At times I don't care where I am or why.
I force myself to work. I try to try.
I long for silence when the whole Fleet's hushed,

But there's no chance of that. I want to hide.
Where can I hide? I don't know what to do,
But do my job, pretending, seeing through
Discharge of duty with a perverse pride

That I'm ashamed of, though it's shared by most.
We sleep-run to our posts to carry out

Tasks for a purpose we don't care about,
Responding to the bugle's brassy boast.

In these, my nightly stanzas, I pretend
To solve and cure myself as each round rhyme
Fits in a sonic sandwich and keeps time
With life, with poetry's clock, as I transcend

What I am meant to do with something else
Subversive, mischievous, not meant for me,
But gleaned from engineering and the sea,
My twin devotions ticking in my pulse.

Nocturnal writing worsens how I feel.
It drives me deeper into melancholy's
Darkness of loneliness and self's disease
Until, through self-disclosure, I touch the real

Predicament of me, what, where I am,
And when, and who, and that is hard and dark,
Selfish and silent on this acrid ark
Where private suffering's ad nauseam

Creates the general climate, not just mine,
Encouraging corruption, fortitude,
Vice, reticence, and drunkenness, a crude
Miscellany of angels, men, and swine,

Although I find that common trinity
In every man I know. Obedient, strong
Somnambulists of action, rubbing along,
We hide our madness under dignity.

XXI

This morning we put out to sea again.
A misfired shell struck *Dmitri Donskoi*.
It hit her bridge, then bounced off like a toy,
Exploding in the sea. *Amen*! *Amen*! –

Prayers from the cruiser sounded hilarious.
Worse, though, were our inaccurate broadsides
Falling far from the targets. Big riptides
Reared in exploding splashes, high as houses.

Harmless in water, but a shell on steel –
Well, that creates a different effect,
Imagination senses. Intellect
Knows little of the new, destructive, real

Power of its own inventions, though they'll know
In Port Arthur (those who've survived, that is)
Technology's fragmenting Nemesis,
Flesh-ripping, ship-sinking, a volcano

In multiples but falling from the sky
In hot, destructive science, imperial
Slaughterers, made to widow, maim, and kill,
One empire wishing that another die.

Surgeons alone possess an intimate,
More morbid knowledge of how H.E. kills,
Those shredding, splintering, modern skills
Which God – if there was one – would prohibit,

Except He hasn't, not ever, not yet,
And isn't likely to. It will get worse,
War's domineering, comprehensive curse,
Deadlier, bigger, without etiquette.

'You may suppose our enemy's fall of shot
More accurate than ours. The evidence,'
Said Rozhestvensky's message, 'makes me wince.
Improve your shooting, or, God knows, we'll rot

'On an oriental seabed, with my ghost
Getting your goat incessantly, my ire
Damning your seamanship and useless fire.
I'll nag you all in Hell. Take that as promised.'

XXII

Letters! Delayed for months, but they've arrived!
In that whirlwind of news and love and kisses
The Fleet became ten thousand privacies.
Its drooping spirits stirred and re-revived

In parcel-opening, only to discover
Mufflers, jumpers, cold-weather underwear.
The Admiralty ought to play us fair!
But thank you, dear. The navy-blue pullover

Will serve me well up north in Vladivostok.
Although addressed to me at the Libau
Anchorage, I'm happy to have it now.
Men read, and then fell silent, nursing shock,

Shame for the Admiralty's incompetence
Or brutal disregard of homesickness.
Indignant, struck with weird paralysis,
But torn, ambivalent, though ages since

They'd tucked in to such post, a big windfall,
Bigger than ever, but because postponed,

They festered, then some wept, while others moaned,
Some laughed, and some did nothing at all.

A little later, controversies broke out.
Our tropical and bug-infested wardroom
Raved in its smoke, as ill-lit as the tomb,
With arguments that left no room for doubt,

So hot-headed they were, and so enraged
One way or another. Do I grow wiser?
Patient, standing aloof, an adviser
(Only when asked), reluctant, disengaged,

I'm no protagonist in this debate
On strategy. I feel that Klado's right,
And wrong. If he were with the Fleet tonight
He'd find a different theme to objurgate

Upon, no doubt at length, the opposite
To what he's printed. If he, too, 'd been starved
Of news and mail, it would at least 've halved
His criticism of us, and inhibit

Apocalyptic forecasts as have maddened
Some in one way and others in another,
Against or for, while this unpleasant bother
Perplexes me, and leaves me saddened.

I do my duty, facing to the front,
And if our lousy, ill-built hull-frames burst
Then it's my duty to repair the worst
Catastrophes that happen, every brunt,

Bash, ram, collision, paltry failure or
Major calamity. But who am I?

I either lose myself or start to die
Or see The Engineer as metaphor

Depicting patriotism or a straight
Obedience to the facts of what we do,
And where we are, and where we're going to,
This end for which we circumnavigate

On a grand scale. But who attends to this?
Who notices the bigness of our visit
To this already raped, colonial planet?
Who sanctioned this colossal pointlessness?

And who am I? And who am I to face
Destructive stasis while a Navy rots
And those who aren't here mount counterplots
Against incompetence? Splice the mainbrace!

XXIII

Disgust, distrust, dismay . . . I can't go on . . .
I sink like a big fat ship into the lap
Ocean projects before me, planet, map,
Mercator's global art, its coloured apron.

Expert at exile, how the Russian mind
Dwells on itself, its introspective craft
As perfect as a Clyde- or Tyne-built crankshaft!
Deft, driven mystics, but we're also blind

To what's outside us, to the practical
But also visionary – *I'd* contend –
Spirit of making. To invent, or mend,
Improve, to make the new, is a miracle

As much as soul-digging's disclosed lyric
Darkness and truth, its rhapsody and song
That diagnose but can't repair what's wrong.
In Russian life all victories are pyrrhic.

But Madagascar's moon re-opens her breast
And her fictitious glitter spills over
Still ships and makes them beautiful, their lover,
Illuminated peace and lunar rest.

And I drift into the dark heart of me
Again, my helpless, Russian, vodka'd heart
Nuts and bolts can't keep from falling apart
On this remote, hot corner of the sea.

XXIV

Say what you like, despair and vodka don't
Drive verse as hard as sheer reality
Peered at and probed until it yields its pity
And all its truths subjected to a count,

Examined, measured, weighed, compared with this,
That, that, that, that . . . until it lives in you,
Writer, and reader, unbearably true
In how it's intimate with what it is.

A boat capsized today and three men drowned.
Letters arrive for dead men, and each day
Sea-burial crews dress in their whites and pray
Into a splash, a weighted corpse's bound,

Melodic, bandaged entrance to the sea's
Airless infinity. An engineer

Knows that the weight's too light for a straight, sheer
Drop to the bottom and the mysteries

Sailors imagine live on the deep seabed.
Such man-boxes will float, and not be still
In the drift of currents – ah, please, be still,
Floating, sinking, increasing Russian dead

Slipped out from under our St Andrew's Cross
Even in death to go to where you're led,
Endlessly descending, floating dead
Describing your resistant, noiseless ethos

In my imagination. Survival!
Sophie, I'm a very unhappy man.
I've stuck to reason, and done all I can,
But the Russian mind 's still mediaeval.

Or mine is. Or I don't know how to cry
Any more. Rational thought, or *how* to think,
Sinks when a reasonable man takes to drink
And Madagascar could be Uruguay

For all I care, or know, or anywhere
As soon as I'm under the spell along with
Everyone else in this Homeric myth,
Even Ignatzius, the debonair

Skipper of the *Suvorov*, who drools over
Famous last glasses in the wardroom's smoke
When we guffaw at what's not quite a joke
And every man feels heroic, a rover,

A salt-sea man of the deep-water Fleet.
For Mother Russia's glory, we're stuck here

Under incompetent command, in a queer,
Unnerving stasis. Waterweeds compete

With barnacles below our waterlines
As local nature grows on us, and grows,
As if we're here for ever or God knows
How long, our inept Admiral's designs

Kept secret to himself, although it's known
He's locked up with the Indian Ocean's charts
Plotting an eastward course, like Buonaparte's
Studious map sessions, shut on his own

With solitude, imperial dreams, and plans.
It's moving east that worries me. My fear
Swims in a bucket of warm, native beer.
Bug-crusted smoke's churned by the turning fans.

XXV

Colonial society, my dear,
Would drive you mad as these French women are.
Despite their resolute *petit bourgeois*
Routines and calling cards on this frontier

Where stays and millinery make no sense,
They still insist on tennis parties, dressed
In all the finery of the self-possessed,
Decked out in a *Parisienne* pretence

That fashion counts in Madagascar where
Tropical heat, rain and mud, alternate with
Drought and dust, and where slow or sudden death
Are facts of which these ladies are aware –

Disease, rebellions, or from sheer despair.
I pity merchants' and officials' wives
Here, in this heat – a squandering of lives
For empire and the chance of Otherwhere.

A Madame Bovary of Nossi-Bé
Flirted with officers. Her husband complained
To the Admiral, but the comedy's stained
With gossip, for I heard the other day

That the Governor's wife has laid the blame
On would-be Emma for our cancelled shore leave.
How like provincial Russia! They deceive
Themselves with the exchange of petty shame

When it's well-known that heavy gambling debts
Run up in Nossi-Bé's straw-roofed casino
Forced Admiral Rozhesvensky to say 'No'
To card games and to primitive roulette

Where officers and men were being skint,
Including me – toot-toot, my dear – Mammon
Being served with all the thrills of backgammon,
In my case, ending up as semi-solvent.

A drama, then, of gossip, thwarted lust.
Torpor, and turpitude, games for high stakes,
Say by themselves that anything that slakes
Ennui's almighty thirsts, or breaks the crust

That boredom bakes around us, will be seized
With hope or gratitude. I understand it,
This need for excess, for extortionate
Pleasures, and I take part; but I'm not eased

As much by gambling as I used to be.
Remember those slow, snow-beamed winter nights
In Yuri's long-windowed house, those Muscovites
At cards, gambling obsessively, elegantly? –

Well, it's not like that! It's more addiction
To the uncertainty that hangs over us
Than social pleasure or a prosperous
Hand of good luck. We're turning into fiction.

XXVI

Vanilla, coffee, leather, coconut oil,
Hardwoods, lemurs for European zoos . . .
When I'm back home with you, I'll write *The Cruise
Of the Second Pacific Squadron*, spoil

A dozen reputations and be a bore
At dinners. I'll be *really* irritating.
I'll be appalling. I'll be *excruciating*.
Among the windbags, I'll be excelsior.

I'll open with, 'Yes, back in nineteen-five
With the Fleet, holed up in stinking Nossi-Bé . . .
Did I ever tell you I'd been down that way?
Yes? Ah! It's down to luck I'm still alive,

'You know, after what I went through down there
In the southern seas. Yes, I've done it all,
Been round the world, and been in battle . . .'
– Dear God, I must be dreaming! – 'Everywhere.

'I've been everywhere. Seen so many things.
Wonders! Strange creatures of both sea and land.

But here's a story I can't understand –
The sailor who stole the church offerings.

'For the life of me, I can't get the hang
Of why he did it. But he did. Confessed,
Indeed. Ashamed. Full of remorse. "No rest
For me, ever," he said. "While those nuns sang,

'"I nicked their box. I'm sorry, sir," he said
Before the special court convened to try
That strange young man, whose tearful, soulful sigh
Shocked me with mystery, his face, his head,

'Sombre with ruin, a most sensitive,
Almost artistic handsomeness. "I drink,"
He said defiantly. "I live to drink.
I beg of you. I don't deserve to live."

'"I'm pleased to hear it," said the President.
"Assuming that the Admiral will ratify
Its judgement, this court rules that you shall die
By firing squad. And that's your punishment."

'I did *not* agree. It didn't get *my* vote.
You gasp? You think it harsh, or think me wrong?
It hardly matters now. I wasn't strong.
On every battleship, torpedo-boat,

'Cruiser, transport, or whatever, officers
Drank like fish, and they didn't have to steal
To do so. They just ran up a big bill
In the wardroom, and that man called them "Sirs".

'The officer presiding, he drank, too.
He drank, and he was drinking when he judged

That petty theft, and he wouldn't be budged.
Indeed, he drank as much, or more, than you' –

And I'll look at someone. 'Forget the death.
I was ashamed, watching the firing squad's
Trembling reluctance to perform as God's
Accessories, takers of life and breath.

'On the first command to fire, they all missed.
That strange young man, he smiled, and held his face,
Somehow – as if he welcomed his disgrace.
It was appropriate that they were pissed.

'The second volley, too . . . The officer
In charge ordered that *all* rifles be loaded
With live rounds, and the firing squad was goaded
And yelled at. It responded with "Yes, Sir!"

'Slobbered and slurred, a kind of mockery,
And there was something almost like tenderness
In how their bullets this time didn't miss
Their handsome target. But what was his story?

'It's the mops I hear, swabbing the gundeck clean,
Washing the blood away, the human stains,
Twelve bullets' worth, heartblood, and the spilled brains.
It's the mops I hear. Do you know what I mean?'

And then I'll go quiet. I'll sink in my chair.
There are those who'll think it's all for effect
And quite beneath their hardnosed intellect.
Later, I'll jump up and shout, '*I've been there!*'

XXVII

Michael, that filthy barber, cut my hair
And trimmed my beard this morning. Holding on,
My dear, to decency, the *sine qua non*
For this decayed, respectable corsair!

Perspiring mightily, he clipped and snipped
With brisk efficiency, his overalls
Reeking of sheer unwashedness, alcohols
(You name it, it was there) and as he quipped –

For, like most barbers, he insists he speak –
His breath hummed of old cabbage soup, the slop
Below-decks have to dine on, then the plop
As globes of sweat dripped from his bulbous beak.

He's good at what he does, though. If only
Our officers and men were half as good
Instead of proud of their ineptitude
I wouldn't feel so frightened or so lonely.

Yes, I'm a prig. I can't get used to it,
This slippage, casual indiscipline
That lets the surface show the life within –
Dilapidated and devoid of wit,

Elegance, style, the poise and self-control
An officer should always show his crew.
If you respect your men, then they'll trust you.
I've men, I know, would trust me with their souls.

On a torpedo-boat this afternoon
The officers were deckchaired and half-dressed
In singlets, showing braces, self-possessed,
Throwing their tidbits to a pet baboon.

The captain lounged barefooted. I noticed
That on one foot there remained a single toe!
The others had been ripped off long ago
In an accident. He got up and pissed

Over the side, and then went back to tea
Under his sun-umbrella, haughty, proud,
As all went dark beneath a thundercloud.
His boat's half-ruined and unfit for sea.

'For God's sake, Flag, why don't you take your tie off?
You'll strangle in this heat. You'll come to grief!
Sit down. Have tea. Or an aperitif?
Give us the gossip from the *Suvorov*.'

XXVIII

Such lightning! Sheets and forks! Tropical rain!
Night suddenly turned day twice in the minute
With fifty ships and flattened forests in it.
Our hot hulls sizzled in the hurricane.

Men stood out on the decks, naked, with soap,
Laughing, jumping, in primitive delight
As lightning made a mockery of night
And rain cooled all with its torrential hope.

XXIX

Poor Nossi-Bé's been Russianized, and we've
Been Nossi-Bé'd. What with twelve thousand men
In a floating city, this French pig-pen
Will know a difference when we're forced to leave.

Beard, barnacles, and such exotic weeds
No one can name them, grow on every hull
Below the waterline, a spectacle
Describing our neglect. Our slowed sea-speeds

Will make us ponderous. What a dirty fleet!
All day, the divers scraped the slimy rind
Of growths and rooted molluscs, but they cleaned
Three square metres. That helmeted athlete

Who leads these submarine Knights of the Sea
Refuses to go back. 'Put her in dry-dock.
Were fifty divers working round the clock
From now to Doomsday, for a fine, fat fee,

'You'd still be barnacled, you'd still be socked
In weed and shell. Best we can do is scrape
Your prows, and keep propellers clean, shipshape
And free of stuff, until you get 'em docked.'

Japanese ships will be clean and freshened up
Should we ever get to them. I'm depressed.
The Fleet's exhausted. All it's done is rest.
I watched my hand shake as it held a cup.

    XXX

He calls Japs monkeys. Monkeys he calls Japs.
It's very odd that enemies who've won
Major victories find themselves looked on
As apes. All right, they're not the best of chaps,

I dare say, but the fact is they can fight.
They have a purpose, and they fight to win.

[89]

Ask the Port Arthur Fleet. Ask Kuropatkin.
I curse this place, its stifling days, hot nights,

Sweltering indolence and lassitude
That bring out a slow swagger and such boasts
You'd think their slurred claims were the words of ghosts
Uttered with lazy courage or subdued

By valorous confidence, not what it is.
And what is it? It isn't heroism.
It's yellow forms of anti-semitism –
Aristo-peasant knee-jerk prejudice.

XXXI

Coal, ammunition, soap, and groceries,
Keep us going, and I keep ships afloat.
We're short of this, and very short of that –
I almost wrote 'of course' – but history's

A matter of such boring details. Meat,
Provender, drinking water, salt, and fruits,
Mean more to navies than these heavy boots
Sent out to us. Sailors can serve in bare feet

As well as shod in what we've just received.
Hoping for ammunition, we get coats,
Infantry footwear, furs, and 'Winter Throats' –
Pills for the Arctic Fleet, not us shirtsleeved

(At best) half-clad tropical bluejackets
(Without the jacket, though, except for me,
Still stuck in rigorous formality,
Traditional, correct, or out of my wits).

Today the soup had rice *and* bugs in it.
'Flag, don't be so severe. A caterpillar
Won't hurt you. It's a lovely little filler.
In dining, sir, I'm indiscriminate.

'Why, what's the difference? Bug, or beef, or lamb,
Pork chop, poultry, shank of goat, fish, or horse?
Or are you saying, sir, that bugs are worse,
Somehow, than sausages, or boiled ham?

'God's creatures, sir, and I can eat them all!
So fork that bug to me. I'll eat it up.
The dainties, sir, on which a man can sup,
Are infinite. They fly, they swim, they crawl,

'They creep, they walk, or else they simply grow
On trees, in fields. It's all so simple, Flag.
It's life, you know; but still, some men will gag
On the lower forms. It just goes to show,

'Civilization's all a case of manners,
So-called morality, when what we mean 's
"Fastidiousness". A man can't live on beans
Alone, and engineers can't eat their spanners.

'So, be a darling, Flag, and pass the mustard,
And the vodka. No mustard? Don't pretend . . .
The world is coming to a fucking end!
No mustard? . . . Gentlemen, it's too absurd!

'*No fucking mustard*! No wine's been *decanted*
For weeks! We're lowering our standards, sirs!
No longer gentlemen and officers!'
He stood up, screamed, and on, and on, he ranted

Until they took him out and off to bed.
Typical breakdown, I'd say, having seen
Several now. As always, an unclean
Sensation lasts with me, the touch of dread

That I, too, might crack up, the way he did,
Diminish, go to pieces, fall apart,
Twitch, scream, dwindle, spout nonsense from the heart,
Waving my arms about like a harpooned squid.

XXXII

Now that my age is one in which months pass
Without you, days go by like years, my love,
In this tub-world we call the *Suvorov* –
A ship named for a soldier! – and the wrasse

(Fish, if you're wondering, that live in wrecks)
Get caught and eaten by unsuperstitious
Mariners. The sea's a slaughterhouse
Sordid with predators, and the non-ethics

Nature thrives on, which mere men imitate.
'I can't eat this! I don't know *who* it's eaten!'
Ignatzius's truculence would sweeten
Any wardroom table, pushing his plate

Away, while he describes a sailor's lore
And younger listeners cough with disbelief
At tales of monsters, or the phantom reef,
Nude mermaids guarding Davy Jones's Locker.

In came a Duty Officer's report
To say men had been caught eating a monkey!

Death-fish and simians, then, on the same day!
Good Captain Ignatzius, holding court,

As usual, over lunch, deplored the case,
Ranting at landlubbers, Admiralty fools
Who can't fulfil such fundamental rules
As those of provisioning. 'It's a disgrace!

'It isn't civilized that men are forced
To guzzle lemurs, or else go without
Meat and victuals, and all because some lout
Well-paid behind a desk just can't be arsed

'To do the needful! It would make you puke,
The way they disrespect us, forcing us
To take the brunt of blame. Preposterous!
When we get home, one of you, *write a book*

'That shows them up. For God's sake, *someone* do it!
And if you do, then, darling, I'll review it!'

XXXIII

Can you imagine how it feels to hold a cube
Of ice on the palm of your hand in this heat?
Skin dreams of snow and winter, rain, and sleet,
Of a cold morning, dressed in a bathrobe,

Shivering in the steam. Better still, though,
A glass of lemonade with lots of ice! . . .
I gasped, and sank within myself. *That's nice!*
I said aloud, to no one, the cold glow

Internalized, refreshment's shock, its kick
In the mouth, Arctic kiss, the joy of frost

Boosting me up with a Russian riposte
To Madagascar's cheese-air and its thick

Humidity, its sweaty cloak, its hot
Tropical tortures for whoever knows
Pleasures of winter rime and cold, deep snows
Or the winter-scent of a coffee-pot

On a stove. But, my dear, I thought of you,
Delightedly, as my chilled drink coursed through
All me, from scalp to toe, from cap to shoe,
O love, love, love, I've lost whatever clue

That I might follow that leads back to you
Unless these letters to you can get through
Mail miles, such distances, such wolves of time
Over which travels my exhausted rhyme.

XXXIV

Forty-two ships of ours now languish here
At Nossi-Bé, twelve thousand men, and ships
Beneath St Andrew's Cross, a flag that grips
The warm wind. Weeds, glued barnacles, and fear,

Cling to us, grow on us. But I've just heard
Where cigarettes are being sold – expensive
As they are, I need to smoke, or I can't live
Without tobacco's constant hummingbird

Across my brain. So, in a smoke-filled room
In the *Aurora*, knocking back the kvass
Sent out in quantity, glass after glass,
We talked of warfare, tactics, guns, and doom.

Most of *Aurora*'s officers believe
We won't steam further East, but must turn back.
'It's a disgrace. This improvised, kulak
Armada's led by dolts on the *qui vive*

'In the Admiralty, by distant half-wits,
Yachtsmen at best, who've never been to sea,
But like to play with maps and strategy
Between society balls and the Tsar's banquets.'

And yes, everything they said rang true
To me, but Rozhestvensky won't turn back,
Because he can't. That warped insomniac
Would steam round the globe – Honolulu,

Calcutta, Santiago, San Diego,
Buenos Aires, Glasgow, Bristol, Cadiz,
Marseille, or anywhere the ocean is,
Greenland, or Tierra del Fuego –

Rather than quit, go home, and compromise
Honour and destiny. Why can't men see
Our Admiral's in love with history
And bigness, with sheer scale, and with the size

Of the possible event? Men's lives at stake
Mean little to him, but his honour's worth –
Our honour, he would say – more than the truth,
And that we need to fight for Russia's sake.

'If he should head for home, I'll eat my cap,'
I said. It must have sounded like the boast
Of someone in the know, instead of lost
For an answer. 'He'll sail us off the map

'Before "surrender", for that's how he sees it.
Or so I think. He's unpredictable
In most things, save his anger, and his will,
And he befriends his fate, and works to please it,

'Unlike the rest of us, who quake to think
What happens when two armoured fleets engage
In modern battle. No one *knows* that rage.
That's why we drink. I'll have another drink,

'Yes, thank you. Generous. Excellent kvass.
It's the uncertainty that makes the bottle
Attractive. That, and the fear of the battle,
Make all of us disciples of the glass.

'Can you guess what I think of most of all?'
Then someone touched my shoulder, gently. 'Tell,
If you want, Flag, but we won't *compel*
You to continue.' So he said, his drawl

As drunken as my own, my reticence –
For which I once was noted – blown apart
By kvass, companionship, a famished heart,
And me too drunk to hold my tongue, and wince.

'Waking with Sophie on a Sunday, sniffing
Aromas of coffee, and kissing her,
Loving her' – sighs from every officer
Around the table, and much handkerchiefing –

Moist eyes, and charging glasses, toasting wives,
Sweethearts, fiancées, or the girl next door,
A lusted cousin or remembered whore –
Drinking away the worst days of our lives.

XXXV

I got your one-word telegram today –
'*Well*.' Couldn't you have said more than just 'Well'?
I can't complain, my dear. But where I dwell
In this hot, humid and remote cranny,

Intimate news would be more welcome than
'Well', and only 'Well.' Did they limit you
To one word only? I could misconstrue
So brief a message, darling, but I scan

Your monosyllable, your one-word song
To me, your poem, and it feels like truth.
I want to go back to our mutual youth
And our hand-holding days of the lifelong

Pledges and kisses, all our promises,
On which my sore profession intervenes
With all those challenges history preens
Itself on, absences, and the abyss

War and geography impose on us.
I long for children – here I go again,
Making things worse, dreaming my unborn son,
My unborn daughter, in this poisonous

Nocturne of noises. One word. '*Well*.' All night
Time's snored and scratched itself through fretful sleep,
And fleecy air makes the warm bulkheads weep
Metal moisture. I dream, and doze, and write.

XXXVI

Each day I write a little, passing time
By keeping time, dreaming of you and home

To tocks of my internal metronome
And, now and then, the cuddle of a rhyme.

Apart from '*Well*' (I'll say no more of that)
Our Admiralty's failed to forward mail.
You should have heard Ignatzius bewail –
'Enough to make a man a democrat!' –

Deskbound incompetence, sheer disrespect,
Official condescension. How he roared!
Irtish arrived, but had no mail aboard,
And we were livid at such crude neglect –

No letters, comforts, and no cigarettes.
But bad news travels fast and free, on wings
As busy as the pain from which it springs,
Speeding from Mukden, gossiped by gazettes

On routes of rumour steaming from northeast.
Poor Russia, when will all your sorrows end?
No mail, bad news, together they portend
Our fate, a fleet that's well and truly fleeced

By its own Admiralty and a State
Careless of casualties and what war costs
In terms of disaffections, tears, and ghosts
Too many for a man to contemplate

Especially as – so the signs all seem to read –
We'll soon be heading up that way, the course
Determined, and the task to reinforce
Hopelessness. Ah, Russia! You mislead

Yourself, or else you're just misled. My heart
Breaks on this wandering and wasteful cruise

Into the depths of overwork and booze,
The depths and dregs of my nocturnal art.

XXXVII

Our drizzled drama's curtain falls as rain
On sizzling ships, so that the decks run black
In mineral streams from deck-heaped coal, each stack
Shedding its gritty coal-dust, grain by grain.

Deck-tethered oxen blather in their stalls.
Khomiakov's crocodile strains on its leash.
It isn't rain so much as its pastiche,
This almost-rain, warm, wet, that hardly falls

So much as drifts, but steady in its soak.
Its perfect lethargy submerges us
In weather-sweat, indolently hydrous
Forms of movement, breaststroking through wet smoke.

I'd rather it were snow, that white sublime
On fields and forests, where each sculpted birch
Encourages a private, white research
That persecutes us with the end of time

Perceived in all that whitened twiggery's
Beauty of before-world, a reaching out,
And reaching in, so far, so deep, that doubt
Blooms in the wonder of its allegories.

XXXVIII

I wonder what you know. My horoscope,
No doubt, 's been cast for you, or cast by you.

Your superstitions could turn out as true
As science, as a figurative hope,

A stab at fore-knowledge. I've thought of this,
Thinking of how I watched the *Suvorov*
Being built, a ship I couldn't say I love,
And didn't then, but here I am, clueless

In Nossi-Bé and strolling down her deck
Avoiding coal-stacks, pondering a hint
From destiny, a stale presentiment –
A buzz in the scalp, a crick in my neck –

That who I am 's bound up with her, her fate
My fate, her 'stars', as you would say, my stars,
Both of us served by your astrologers,
Our lachrymose and superstitious State.

XXXIX

There's often less to do than one supposes,
Or so I find; and then I find there's *more*,
Much more, to make a man exhausted, or
Impatient with his lot, his daily doses

Among broken machinery, ill-tended
Gear and engines, best thrown over the side
Instead of tentatively fixed. What pride
In me insists that disrepair be mended

When I can't mend myself, and work be done
When all I do depends on other men
Who don't work well, so that I'll do again,
All over, once again, in the hot sun?

Any clown can tell, though, that our course is set
For somewhere, for there's so much work to do,
And engineers are doing it, those few
Competent hands among us, but who get

No thanks from dilettante landsmen, those
Ratings and officers who can't yet feel
A voyage through their fingers or the real
Hubbub of preparation through the nose

As, almost surreptitiously, our ships
Get ready for wherever we must sail.
Those who suspect are posting off their mail,
As I will, dear, and seal this with my lips,

My kiss, my love, my wet lips on French gum,
My tongue, my kiss, my love, my spit, my wet
Amorousness. For how can I forget?
Cut carefully. Taste Malagasy rum.

Taste me as how I am these days without you.
We could head home. But I don't think we will.
It's off to war for us, my love, but I'll
Dream you dream me, and dream, and dream about you.

PART SIX

I

You haunt my poem, the way a woman should
Inhabit her husband's verses. Yes, yes,
We've put to sea. Eastern geographies
Stretch before us, part-charted on the nude

Indian Ocean, miles and miles of tears
And sweat for me, and all my sweet devoirs
Directed at imagined moon and stars
Caught in a birch branch for a hundred years.

To find a glimpse of who I am, or what,
I'll have to swallow Russia and a sea.
Each verst of water looks the same to me,
Like walking on the steppes, from one named spot

To one named spot, to one named spot, the same
And endlessly the same, an onion-steepled
Toy landmark hinting that the place is peopled,
Though only those who live there say its name

Other than tax-collectors. Here, Ocean is
Uncharted, unpoliced. It's not a 'here',
Or place. It's a nowhere. It isn't fear
Forces me say this, this big notionless

Wonder that wet space should be so spacious
Now that no land's in sight, and I'm cut free
From earth again, let loose, and this vast sea
My element, an endlessly audacious

Physics and meditation for the eye
And soul. Not fear, but welcome to such space
And welcome, welcome, to the salt no-place
Where the unbirded winds intensify

Existence to the tip of an extreme
And any time it's silent its silence is
Sinister, sudden, unexpectedness
Dwarfing all senses, an unuttered scream.

II

Sky drained of poetry, I watched the dawn,
Chewing my third orange – tart, not quite ripe,
The way I like them. Steam from a burst pipe
Whistled its grey one-note and woebegone

Lament of punctured power. Artificers
Approached it hopelessly, with the wrong tools,
Still half asleep. Ignatzius ridicules
Our untrained crews, 'unwitting saboteurs'

(As he calls them). Here on *Kamchatka*, though,
They're good and willing lads, eager to learn,
And I can teach them, though it's hard to turn
A village carpenter to one who'll know

In future how to fix a Kingston valve.
Kamchatka's flooded engine-room took six
Wet, squalid, oily hours of toil to fix,
But we did it. I thought we might dissolve,

So wet we were, holding our noses as
We dipped, searching for valves to turn off

In the *Kamchatka*'s over-flooded trough
Of an engine-room, our spit, shit and piss

Only too obvious in the rancid tide.
Kamchatka's skipper said, 'We're sinking, Flag' –
As if I needed to be told! Windbag
Aristocrats, with nowhere left to hide

Now that we're back in harness, strut the decks
In all their old incompetence, their pride
Well polished but their skill undignified,
Their ships already like as many wrecks.

Our speed's that of the slowest – five knots, or eight
In a good spell, and then we have to stop
For some breakage or other. Sea-anchors drop
And forty-two ships are obliged to wait

While I dash to the culprit, there to do
Whatever labour 's needed to repair
Strain on our ill-designed, old-fashioned gear.
I'm quick at writing, but there will be few

Spare hours from now to Doomsday or whenever.
I can't do without this, though. Who'd have thought it? –
Me, a versifying, night-time, proper poet!
Let's keep it secret, this, my salt endeavour

Completely out of character. The sea
Inhabits me, and I inhabit it.
Ignatzius spouts and quotes, honing his wit
On me, his chosen philistine, on me,

Who spends the locked night writing up the day
With all of Russian poetry inside me

And Homer and Camões right beside me,
And engineering, terror, poetry.

III

Fear gnaws at some men's innards. You can tell
By how they watch the sea's shape-shifting size
And infinite deceptions tyrannize
The eye with loneliness and miles of swell

Heaving moodily. Such melancholy miles!
Such clouds, such weather, and such dreary space
Recorded on the features of a face
Ashen with hopelessness . . . No desert isles!

No Crusoe-havens for our suicides
Slipped overboard into a turbulent
Last minute of waving, and one last squint
At light and life . . .

Don't close the rhyme! I've seen all this before
But can't get used to it, can't get blasé –
'Oho! Another coward jumped today!'
It is to enter salt, to go through a door

In a grain of it, into the universe,
Not out of it as some men choose to think.
Correct, too, that they call the sea 'the drink'.
For that's what gets to them. It really hurts.

I'd give much for a long day in a garden,
Or take a walk, anywhere in Europe,
With you, my dear, and something nice to sup
At dusk in a gazebo when leaves harden

Against the last light as the birds hurry
Into their strange silence and feathered sleep
That always seems so touching and so deep.
And right now, I could do with a strawberry,

Or twenty, doused in vodka, sugar, cream
(Remember Bonn?) with the moon falling on
Your hair, and when the tiresome day has gone,
Night in your arms, and love at its extreme.

IV

I get that scent of somewhere else again,
Our apartment. It's a fragrance of us,
Our clothes, our soap, us, and our amorousness
In days before this world without women.

It comes out of the blue – literal blue,
Tropical blue. I can be rowed across
Oceanic swell to a near dead-loss
Mechanical failure when scents of you

Smite me while I sit oilskinned at the prow
Facing the sun with salt-spray on my face.
Hundreds of miles from land and commonplace
Emergencies. Deep in the middlebrow

Dangers of engineering, I find out
About myself, and poetry, and us,
And Russia, the atrabilious
Vehemence of self-knowledge and self-doubt,

Identity's passions, and who I am,
Precisely, what I do, exactly that

Among my stern machines, my habitat
Below-decks with the hulls and boilers. Damn

All Tsars and Admirals, all 'strategists'
And would-be conquerors who waved us off
Into the stagnant pride of Romanov,
The hankies waving from so many wrists

It looked liked massed surrender – so it seems
After so many months, and men made crude,
Ironic, bitter, from the solitude
That rises from within, corrupting dreams,

Making everything strange.
                                        Get on with it!
Admire the dolphins or the Manta Ray,
The blowing whales, the blueness of the day . . .
The frail, enfeebled nerve that's mother-wit.

V

This Fleet eats coal mines. Coaling! It's the worst.
It's not the toil, Sophie, but that I'm cursed
With more work than one man can do, while he,
That angry, raging fool, our C-in-C,

This Rozhesvensky, howls at each delay,
And yells at me, and calls *me* for a fool,
When *he's* the master of the Fleet's misrule,
Lord of its future and its day-to-day

Mismanagement. Demoralized, we slog
And grumble, dutiful, but hoping for
Thanks, or encouragement, nothing much more,
While wondering what *he's* writing in his log.

Rumour has it – from his aide-de-camp – we're
Not exactly lost, but no one knows we're here
(Wherever 'here' is) on the charts of fear
Leading to bloody battle God-knows-where.

VI

Sailing small boats. They ride low in the sea,
Always unsafe, not under man's control
On a violent cradle's surge and roll
Fastened for ever to its energy.

But in mid-ocean, on a smaller vessel,
That's when you feel its mindless strength, its heaves,
Varieties, the way it interweaves,
An infinitely interlocking wrestle

With itself, never sleeping, staying true
To its identities of deep and wet,
Its whole simplicity, with no regret,
Remorse, ethics, for what it does to you.

Why do I love it when the sea's the stuff
Floods all my present life with work and grief?
And yet I'd give much for a new birch-leaf
Bursting out of the gardened Spring's rebuff

To winter, or, in landlocked Samarkand,
Flowers round a fountain when the morning's fresh
And watered breezes play around my flesh.
The truth is that I love both sea and land.

I think the truth is that I love too much.
A heart can only love as much as heart

Can love. I'm not a saint. I drink, and fart.
I lie at night, and imitate your touch.

The way a sky can sink into the sea
And colour it! The many shades of blue! –
Grey-white, white-grey, gold, green, and every hue
Between now and the rainbow, all for me!

VII

It's odd, that in a 'modern' Fleet – so called –
We've had to improvise lookouts' crow's-nests
With barrels and cages on our cruisers' masts.
What these lads see is probably doubled –

They're given vodka, then they're hoisted up
To scan the far horizon and the sea's
Promise of peril and of mysteries,
Pissed in a barrel at the main mast-top.

East Indies, ahoy! But there's nothing there.
Only the bare sea. Only that nothingness
That is distance, nude miles, and the caress
Emptiness grants us when there is no 'where'

To point to. My knowledge, lacking that fact
Called 'destination', or called 'destiny',
Explains the way I am. Self-scrutiny,
Such as it is, just leaves me inexact,

Puzzled, and curious. I want to know
What happens next, though I already know
Tomorrow's labour will be my tomorrow,
And, for a time at least, each day's tomorrow

Succeeds the day before, the same old way,
With toil, slog, insult, orders, and commands,
Ache in my heart and limbs, grease on my hands,
My uniform in chronic disarray.

We've all been through our introspective moods
Before. Even the heartiest dig deep in
Mind, self, and loneliness. It's what we're steeped in.
A Fleet's made of multiple solitudes

When it's as far from home as we are now.
Thousands of dreams afloat, and yet these dreams
Devise a silence of so many screams
Withheld by honest men who don't know how

To share their sorrows. Let them go unsaid,
Half-said, or kept as secrets as we sail
Over uncharted waters on our frail
Iron- and steel-clad and full-steam-ahead

Argosy to nowhere we've been told about.
At night the balalaikas play, and songs
Give full voice to our sorrows and our wrongs.
But there's no scream, and no defiant shout.

VIII

The twentieth century. I think of change
Between the birth of Pushkin and Chekhov's death.
The nineteenth century, the twentieth –
To ponder so much time is to derange

A brain already battered by too much
Work and anxiety. Ignatzius claims

That literature's our anchor, and then names
His favourite poets. Poetry's a crutch,

Though. Mystical, melodic, it can't teach
A nation how to fight a modern war.
They tell us what we might be dying for,
But that's just courage, love, and overreach

Into anachronism. Ignatzius speaks
As if incompetence and poetry
Ennoble Russia's abject helotry
Or justify our status as antiques

Before the scientifically wise,
Astute and calculating Japanese,
Mocked by our men as 'apes', a sub-species
Disgusting for their zest and enterprise

While we outdo them vastly in virtues
Learned on the ballroom floor, our etiquette
As European as our National Debt,
Abhorring anything that smacks of news.

'Perhaps', and 'anyhow', our 'ifs' and 'buts',
Procrastinations, muddles, and mistakes,
Could see us through this war. But my heart quakes
For what lies up ahead, when the door shuts

On our old-fashionedness, and opens on
Modernity and new destructiveness
In ten- and twelve-inch armour-piercing kisses
And what was floating suddenly is gone

Beneath the waves. Who wouldn't be afraid
When faced with what no Fleet has faced before,

The open sea's first taste of modern war?
Adrift, unrescued, broken, and dismayed,

The mind can't take it in. 'Then just don't think,'
Ignatzius says. 'And don't imagine it.
In any case, we'll have our chance to win it.
Why not? Brave fellows all! Here, have a drink.'

IX

While marksmen scan the clear and moving sea
For signs of danger, divers work among
Massing sharks, perched on an iron rung
On lowered ladders, as, unnervingly,

From underwater ring the blows of hammers
On *Gromky*'s broken rudder. Such a noise!
Like singing, or the sound of the turquoise
Water . . . It's as if the Ocean clamours

For our attention, or, at least, for mine.
Pretending to take notes on these repairs
I'm jotting this instead, though it's like prayers
For divers threatened in the turquoise brine

By sea-teeth, by the death that swims in salt
With the emphatic splendour such as sharks
Display, sleek, dentate Tsars, the sea's autarchs,
Mystical, terrible, and nature's fault.

X

When Yuri died – the summer after we met,
My dear, and I know that you'll remember

My talk about him – then come November
His unharvested orchard was a wet

Apple-squalor. The almost-molten fruit,
Frosted in glinting lumps, gave off a scent
I can't forget, and it came back to haunt
His old friend tonight. I walked there. Underfoot,

First there was the crisp snap of frosted skin
Followed by squelches, then that sweet release
As apple-odour's olfactory masterpiece
Shocked memory with what was locked within

A ten-year friendship with a leisured man
Whose horticultural passions outlived him
By one cold season's brutal interim
Until his brother and a courtesan

Moved into his Muscovian estate.
Devoted to pleasure, vodka, and 'wit',
First they neglected, then they ruined it.
I went there once. It filled my heart with hate.

For I remembered, as I do tonight,
Such scent of apples, such fragrance of him
From his wasted orchard, as if a whim
Or whiff of past times turned smell into sight

As Yuri walked across my sniffing eye,
My seeing sense of smell, my upside-down
Sensory apparatus. And me, grief's clown,
All I could do was sniff, and step, and cry,

Which is what I do now for my dead friend,
Pacing my tiny cabin, holding on

To whatever virtue lives in writing down
Truth, mood, and mind, and what I comprehend

As friendship at its utmost, Yuri, and me,
Talking of love and friendship half the night,
And he the one who yearned the most to write,
And me the one who longed to go to sea!

XI

Work, reverie, work, write, sleep, ablute . . .
Routines and days. Golovko's oh-so-slower.
Though never quick, he's slower now than ever.
Today, though, he remembered to salute,

And it surprised me – I don't ask for it.
The slightest nod or tiniest bow will do
To keep up the appearance of what's due
Between an officer and opposite.

It's the change in him that perplexes me,
His deferential woes, his big 'Sorry',
As if he lives always in constant worry –
And all the world's children lost at sea.

'I miss my son and daughter, sir. It's sore
On any father to be far away
And not to be beside them when they play,
The way we used to, on the Neva's shore.

'I get confused, sir, for I feel I've failed
My family by being here with the Fleet
When I'm not there to make sure that they eat,
For they've grown poorer by each mile we've sailed.'

XII

For days and nights, I've tried – God knows, I've tried
To write my mind. I can't make sense of me
Dwarfed by monotonies of sky and sea.
It leaves me feeling unidentified

Or nameless on the oceans we pollute
With waste, this lovely emptiness, the sheer
Reductive paradox of its grandeur.
Our coals patrol the sky on wings of soot.

To describe the Ocean, you must write with it.
To write my mind, then I must write with it.
My worthless life means I must write with it.
As for my terror, I must write with it.

I must write with my love, with all of me.
Strange, Sophie! Me! This woeful mariner's
Signed up as one of poetry's beginners! . . .
I don't know why. Vodka, or else the Sea,

Or maybe just an ambush in my blood
Waiting to happen, turning it to ink
Out of the hurt of something (love, sea, drink)
And then this gush, this most pathetic flood

Missing the main gist of my state of mind
Which I can't bring myself to speak aloud
As if it's something to be disavowed
Or better left unwritten and unsigned.

But still, I want to say it. I want to speak
Out of a strong or still unbroken heart
In simple language, but with words of art,
To say that I, too, live, that I'm unique,

An individual, reduced to these
Dithering descriptions, but still, I write
Out of my love for you, the world, day, and night,
Out of my sorrow. I don't write to please,

But to be truthful. I believe in truth.
(Perhaps that *is* my mind.) Great waves roll on
Across the blue, an hour after dawn –
Infinite, planetary, universal broth.

My mind's unsaid. Seepage will see me through.
I'll let it leak, if I can't let it speak.
Whispers are better than a mindless shriek
Any day of the week, and on this blue

Tilt of the sea and sky, human dilemmas
Amount to mortal trivia, as weak
And squalid set before Ocean's mystique,
Its vast nursery of the ethicless.

XIII

For almost fifteen minutes in the night,
As I leant on the rail, the lamp swayed
Over tarpaulin'd coal, and someone played
A sad old song on the piano. Moonlight

Perused the Ocean. Lunar loveliness
Promoted my quarter hour of whole peace.
I blew smoke, then my smoke seemed to increase
In the great puffs from our stacks. Relentless,

We steam ahead. I watched our argosy
Behind us. Its trail of lights contested

Illumination with a sky congested
With stars, the dominant Moon, the sea

A yellow basin and as calm as glass
Despite our clumsy presence. Man-made weight,
Numbers, and strength, try to intimidate
Nature, but can't. The elements surpass

Even the cleverness of engineering,
Which imitates, competes, creates, constructs.
For all its ships, machines, and viaducts,
Progress, and kindness, just out of hearing

I almost heard, or thought I almost heard,
A voice of Moon and Ocean telling me
No nautical machine can trump the Sea.
It was the moonlight's side- or afterword

Proposed against our incandescent wash
And half-still flag at the stern, the long Fleet
Strung out behind us like a city street
Inhabited by invisible big fish

Native to these parts. Nocturnal fishers
Cast lines and lures and trawl into the deep abyss
Beyond all sounding in the fathomlessness
Where monsters live. I'm one of their wellwishers.

I like to eat fresh fish. It makes me feel
Maritime, knowing one day they'll eat me,
A sailor dined on, digested by the sea,
All gluttony repented, and our steel

Turned into sunkenness. Morbidity!
I've come so far now and don't feel afraid

Any longer, not of death, that clichéd
Terror, although I fear my own self-pity.

XIV

Another coaling day, and the black fossil
Released its customary storms of dust.
I thought the air was likely to combust.
Dizzying, the temperature's colossal

Reading went off the scale, and men passed out.
I remembered my Arctic stint, so cold
That I saw young men visibly grow old
While an officer, ordering by shout,

Watched his command turn into flakes of ice.
The bergs and frozen wonders of that place
Would melt in this heat, where a man's grimace
Rasps through the black dust and the sweated price

Coal costs us, hewn, dug, sweated up from mines
In South Wales, sweated off German colliers,
Sweated into bunkers by coal-carriers,
Profit for someone, but the Sun still shines

Like nightmare, and remorselessly it shines
On half-stripped men who yell, and call, and faint,
Cursing the cruel Sun, though the complaint
Falls on the deaf ears of the watching captains.

XV

On board the *Gromky* , a torpedo boat –
They dragged me out of bed at five a.m.

The sea was heaving, swelling, salty phlegm.
The Ocean is our universal moat.

On *Gromky*, yesterday, I thought repairs
Taken well in hand by our divers, but –
Ah, *but*, *but*, *but*! – some fool left valves half-shut.
I might as well work by spells and prayers

As engineering know-how, but at least
Today we lunched decently on sardines
Although the *Gromky*'s notion of cuisine 's
One that knows nothing of an ample feast.

So starved is this boat of provisions for
Its officers and men, it's miserable
Being towed across these swells, seasick and ill,
And every moment one of being at war

Not with the Japanese, but with the sea
And haughty and unamiable neglect
Of which our Admiral 's the architect,
And with discomfort's hunger and ennui.

What work, though, even on a full stomach!
Rolling by more than 25 degrees
The boat dipped as it leaned into the sea's
Momentous turbulence. Divers, seasick,

Battered by hull and rudder, badly beaten
By an unbeatable element, while sharks
Sped in and out of the pocks of rifle-barks . . .
'Haul these men in, before someone gets eaten!'

Yelled one of *Gromky*'s ratings. I agreed,
But . . . but the work had to be done before

Gromky went to the bottom. 'Either/Or . . .
Either we work, or sink – when we'd *all* feed

Sharks, and God knows what other fish might be
Down there waiting!' Or so I said, disgusted
To hear my work questioned and distrusted.
'I don't like it. It doesn't delight me

'To send these good men down to risk their lives
Patching this deathtrap, but at least I, too,
Get wet and filthy, just the same as you.
Let's work, survive, and go home to our wives.'

Resentment? No, don't speak to me of that
Rancid emotion. I'm as disaffected
As any bluejacket who's been suspected
Of subversion, and I'm no diplomat,

Aristocrat, or democrat, but me,
An engineer and amateur of verse
Whose parallel obsessions blend to curse
Each other as a creature of the sea.

XVI

I'm so much older, but I'm still as young
As ever I was, though I grow no wiser,
And suffering, as an antagonizer,
Seems overrated. It ought to go unsung,

Not be the inspiration of our songs
Or source of surrender to fat, sad tunes
Dissolving indignation in the moon's
Blue homesick wash, and all our manic wrongs

Rinsed in an ethos of accepted pain.
No boat was sent to take me off *Gromky*.
I went by whaler on a heaving sea,
Bounced off the *Suvorov*, and grabbed a chain,

Then pressed my boot-soles on its hull and heaved
With and against the angles of its leans
Into the blue-green-black of the Ocean's
Tantrum, then spilled onto the deck, relieved,

Waterlogged, exhausted, only to find
Rozhestvensky's boots on the deck staring me
In the wet face, his voice declaring me
Incompetent and shameful, out of his mind

With autocratic anger. 'You're on the Staff!
Yet you return at five instead of three! –
Covered in filth!' He made a fool of me
Then rounded on Ignatzius. 'Riffraff!

'Ill-bred, ill-mannered, and unfit to serve
His Imperial Majesty. You, keep your eye
On officers and men on this pigsty
Suvorov's become. Three, not five! Your nerve

'Appals me, sir. Now get below. Get washed!'
No use replying when he's in that mood.
I work all day, but where's his gratitude?
I fell asleep, still wet and mackintoshed.

XVII

Yesterday was autumn, but today it's spring.
Who'd cease to be astonished by this planet,

The definite, the known, the infinite?
Science comforts me with its surprising

Discoveries, the way poetry can't
Get through to fact, or the material
Knowledge of substance, true, useful, real,
Workable improvements that cantos can't

Deliver, and never will – that's *their* glory.
A poem measures nothing, but can cure
Diseased time, and make the uncertain sure.
The way a child asks, 'Tell me a story!' . . .

The way a story answers to a child's
Deepest interest! . . . Ah, I remember how
I read of snow, before I saw the snow
For the first time fall on the Muscovian fields,

And dreamt I was dreaming, or else I thought
I might be thinking it, that rhyme of white
With all the wide world on that moonlit night.
What did I learn that night, what was I taught

Far from Tashkent, my mother holding me? –
'See, Eugen,' – she said me in German – 'There!
I think of snow as poetry and prayer.
One day, my son, I'll take you to the sea.'

XVIII

Donskoi reports nocturnal funnel-sparks
On the dark horizon. But why shadow us?
Why bother, when we're so slow and cumbrous
In our barnacled, weather-beaten arks?

The weather's worsened and it's blowing a gale –
A day for broken tow-ropes, broken masts,
Lurching, and cursing like iconoclasts
Among the bumps and breaks and sheer scale

Of the intemperate Ocean, heaving, big
Beyond belief. All of a sudden, I
Trembled before its power. I defy
Anyone not to – shape, weight, of God's swig,

Universal libation, the brine quaff
Soaking me through, my cap swept off, my hair
Rain-and-salt-raddled stuff, *my* disrepair
And such as makes our watching Admiral laugh

At how I get dirty, filthy, as I toil
With salted peasantry, using my hands
At work he can't pretend he understands –
Sea-son, salt-son, not a son of the soil.

XIX

The off-key singing of our drunken officers
Would never be allowed in any fleet
Other than ours. 'It purifies the meat' –
It's true, my dear, intrepid voyagers,

Such as we are, depend on an excuse
For crazy drinking, tippling to excess
Beneath the blurred fans in the Senior Mess,
Where, with my friends, I feel like a recluse

Holding the evening's cognac to the light.
We've fooled the watching world by our bold course

For the Malacca Straits. Telegraphic Morse,
And soon, will tap dot-written news tonight

From the Pulo Way lighthouse when we pass
Under the new moon, and ship after ship
Stun Dutch keepers with numbers. That's why we sip
With thoughtful passion, staring in each glass

As if its chemistry 's something to read,
A private almanac that tells you if you'll live
Or die. Their singing 's what I can't forgive!
But on we creep, an armoured millipede

Several miles long and given to music,
Much prone to alcohol and cabbage soup,
Led by a melancholy nincompoop,
And off to war, then on to Vladivostok.

But not Saigon. We'll stop at Camranh Bay.
I sit and write. The others drink. I drink.
The others sing. I sit and write, and think.
My 'wisdom' touches nothing I can say

Except surrender to the circumstance
In a hope of survival. Do your best
By what you have. Destiny does the rest.
Don't forget love. For that's your only chance.

Through love you can become more than you were.
Romance! Romance! Well, that's 'wisdom' for you.
Nothing sounds triter than what's clearly true.
I might as well listen to the fans purr.

'What's this you're writing, Flag? Why don't you sing?'
'I'm working out how to repair the ailing *Terek*

Before the dear becomes a total wreck,
If you must know. A *very* tricky thing,

'Indeed, I can tell you.' 'God, Flag, your sums,
Your algebra . . . You'll end up gaunt and bald,
And work won't help you when your number's called,
So put your mind away, and join your chums.'

XX

I count the month of miles to Vladivostok
Though life is measured now by cigarettes –
In very short supply. Men run up debts
For a smoke. It's strange, the things they'll hock

For a packet of a tropical brand
Rolled in colonial factories - *Guyane*,
Cannibal Puff, or *Métropolitain*.
Tobacco 's imperial. It's the suntanned

Planter's delight, along with ebony,
Ivory, rubber, cotton, spices, hides,
Furs, fisheries, though what a land provides
Means nothing if there just aren't any

Where you happen to be, and you want them.
French cigarettes – I'm down to my last hundred –
Made me sleepy. I know now why they did.
These sweet colonial puffs have opium in them.

Money can't buy them now. I've hidden mine
Well-wrapped in oilcloth to keep them dry.
I'll eke them out and smoke them on the sly,
My soporifics, my chance of benign,

Full-dreaming, irresponsible slumbers
Remote from poetry or engineering
Where all this armoured gondoliering
Gets beaten by pure, more radiant numbers.

PART SEVEN

I

Two Oceans crossed! Now the Malacca Straits
Will lead us south past Singapore, then round
Up the South China Sea on a northbound
Destiny, on which no one speculates,

At least openly, although men's private thoughts
Feel almost audible. It's all a game,
A masquerade of fear, hiding our shame
In the behaviour of brave Argonauts

Facing a sure Medusa up ahead
Or round a coastal corner in the night
Where suddenly the world explodes in light,
Noise, pain, and terror. Then you're dead.

Is that how it will be? It sounds silly
To think about how and why one might die;
But I know it's common – the way men cry
In their sleep, as if, momentarily,

They let their secrets loose in hot cabins
Or crowded lower decks in the vain hope
Someone who hears might teach them how to cope
Or cure their woes with secret medicines.

II

I've arrived at history. I always knew,
From day one, all along, I was in it.

Time is incurable and not a minute
Goes back to where and when it was the true

Happiness of our lives. The verb of love
Whose energies look for me in the dark
Seems less like poetry than a chance remark
Half-overheard deep in the *Suvorov*.

Malacca's coastal lights reminded me
Civilization's both fact and a dream.
A searchlight caught a schooner in its beam –
White, tidy, and its beauty blinded me

With maritime perfection, my boyhood
Vision of going and discovery,
That old adventure, fun, and reverie
Supped in the grass in bookish solitude.

And come to this – not on a white schooner
But, battered, barnacled, a battleship
Beset by nipping coal dust, where valves drip,
Then burst, and where tonight is truly lunar

Looking at a coastal town, and the white sails,
White hull of a boy's dream. But what boys dream,
Out of boys' books, becomes a quinquereme
Of monstrous, modern steel; and time regales

Boy-men and men-boys with its ironies,
Terrors, nostalgias. But time is pure –
For what it does or doesn't do, no cure,
Only what happens, and only what is.

III

'Why are we here? What are we searching for?' –
He stared me in the eye, a holy fool
Adept in all the arts of ridicule.
'We've volunteered to spoon the soup of terror.'

Unbarbered hair, unshaven, red-eyed, gaunt,
One such as only Russia produces,
Our hellfire race of rakes and mad recluses.
And there was Singapore, its waterfront

Crowded with the curious. It didn't exist
For him, for far too long lost in a brain
Devoted to a high, spiritual plane,
Part priest, part madman, and part anarchist.

He placed his hand on my knee; I recoiled.
It was as if I entered his laughter.
'There is no now. There's only the hereafter.'
I was afraid of him – unkempt, gargoyled.

Can you believe it? He'd driven a nail
Through his foot, into the deck, and blood oozed
From his fixed boot. He laughed at me, amused
By my shock, by the big, unuttered yell

Formed on the O of my mouth. 'Ah, terror!'
He said. 'That's what we're looking for. We dream
Ourselves towards the worst that makes us scream
And Life/Death is no choice, no either/or,

'But only what is, and it's purest pain
In the last moment of ordeal, the last
Split-second where we turn into the past
Of us, at the extreme of the profane

'Before becoming spirit.' I nodded
At this nonsense, though worried by its truth –
The waste of life and time, the waste of youth –
As if my Slav soul, too, felt itself prodded

By barbarous antiquity, by God
As God is known among our pious race,
Our praying multitudes who know their place
Means 'on your knees', ruled by incense and rod

And by a mystic code that no one knows
Exactly how – or if it's wise – to crack it.
The rational eludes us. We lack it.
We hide in our corners, in the shadows

Where candles dwindle. Bluejacket police
Arrived, a rifle-and-bayonet squad
Seeking a hirsute fantasy of God
With a nail through his foot, a masterpiece

From the studio of Russian madness.
Their escapee, they rifle-butted him
On the mouth as he tried out his 'wisdom',
And slapped their cuffs on, then found out his

Foot was affixed to the deck. They called for
A claw-hammer, and then the blood-filled boot
Was set free from the deck. That bloody boot
And puddle, I took as a metaphor

Of something or other – but I'm not sure
What it figures. Enslavement to our race?
Our infinite rebelliousness? Disgrace
That we're so big, and yet so very poor?

An empire dedicated to its notion
Of itself, its spirit, its strange mystique,
Its size and scope, its sense that it's unique?
Or is it just a consequence of Ocean,

Too many days and nights spent on the sea?
It addles men, and makes the mystic proud,
So that they try to say their souls aloud.
Of course, this never could apply to me!

IV

Now Nebogatov's left Djibouti, war
Feels closer than it's ever felt before.
It's as if some half-wit 's opened a black door,
The Office of the Forbidden Thoughts, or

Time 's put a stop to all tranquillity,
Benevolence, sound sleep, and peace of mind.
By choosing sides, Time's disinclined
To be neutral. It's chosen hostility.

For Nebogatov's Third Pacific Squadron 's
Made up from dockyard relics, thrown together,
Archeological, birds of a feather,
Weather-beaten, patched, rust-scraped veterans.

Four days of false alarms! The Japanese
Either out-sail our scouts, or they're not there,
Or rumoured cleverly as everywhere
As part of a colossal, lethal tease.

V

Coastal mists at Camranh Bay covered crags
Reluctant to be blotted out, too high
In any case, protected by the sky.
But it was beautiful. Imagination gags

On the *real* astonishment of places, real
Planetary gardens, waters, coastal mists,
Such as affright my heart, this sensualist's
Inherited demand for the ideal.

I wiped tears from my eyes before such beauty –
A landfall such as met my heart's desire!
It was for this I went to sea, on fire
With love of ships and miles, the new, and duty.

And it was 'duty' led me to add up
Hellish figures. From Nossi-Bé to Camranh,
Four thousand and five hundred sea miles! Man
Flays flesh, flays nerve, and love, as, cup by cup,

Liquor sustains the journey and the quest.
One hundred and twelve times we had to stop
On our sea-march, stop, stop, and hop, and hop,
The great weight of us. Like something unblessed

By nature, but by seventy-odd priests,
Somehow we made the trip – twenty-eight days
Before we touched on land! And then this haze,
Magical mists hiding the French Far East's

Promise of Annamite pleasures, of food
And drink. A run ashore 's out of the question.
So there's a blow to my agog digestion,
My hunger, and my thirst, my landward mood,

For, frankly, I would like to take a walk
Among trees and pagodas, and among
Flowers, women, children, the reek of ox-dung,
Earth-smells, the always-startling song or squawk

That new birds make from unfamiliar leaves
On unfamiliar trees, and standing still,
Above all, standing still, standing until
The light of the immobile earth achieves

Its moon and stars. And there were seventy-three
Stops made for steering-gear or engine-room
Calamities. Hence my exhausted gloom,
For our clapped-out machinery means me.

VI

Outside the bay, a heron and a dove
Fell on the decks of *Kniaz Suvorov*.
What omen's this then, coming from above?
What mad Annunciation? What God-love

Shown by the drop of birds? The heron died.
A thoughtless boot kicked it over the side.
Wings stretched, it tumbled on the strong riptide.
But cradled in gloved hands, and pacified

By a kind midshipman (no more than a boy)
The dove recovered, and it flew away
Into the fading light on Camranh Bay.
I breathed again, my love, relieved by joy.

VII

A cruiser named for a philosopher! –
Descartes! Unthinkable in our Navy!
Our ships are named for warriors, wavy-
Mustachio'd Tsars, Admirals, metaphor.

I wonder what that rationalist would think
Were he to spend a few days as our guest
In the wardroom? He'd find us overdressed,
But not too clean? And far too fond of drink?

And too religiose? I'm in no doubt
Our French philosopher would sniff our taste
For incense and our blatantly two-faced
Approach to everything. He'd find us out.

As so does *Descartes*'s Admiral Jonquières.
Despite his courtesies, he's witness to
All sorts of rammings, breakdowns, impromptu
Patchings, repairs, mayhem, as officers

And ratings scud from zest to indolence,
From discipline to insubordinate rest
Amidst the foggy coaldust. Unimpressed,
The Frenchman smiles, and bows his compliments,

Lauding our 'epic voyage'. But I winced
To overhear such flattery, such praise
For what may well be true, for the truth weighs
Like bitter judgement on the unconvinced

Who've brought the Fleet this far against the odds
Dictated by the Admiralty and Admirals
More than our scapegoat saboteurs and rebels.
It's not French praise we want. We lack the Gods

Of miles and Oceans to applaud our quest
Into an alien or false tradition,
Searching for victory, duty, perdition,
And rounding to the east out of the west.

Although our Empire landwardly possesses
Both compass points, by sea it means a trudge
Through tons of coal and hellish smoke, a smudge
Such as would smear the world's caresses

With the besmirch of April, 1905,
Our recent century. Apocalypse
Never was my forte! – Too many ships
To look after, trying to stay alive

As an Engineer, and as a man who thinks,
Who prays like this: 'Dear clock, heal this. Please heal.
Please heal the century and what I feel
Heads towards us.' The probable shrinks

Into the likely, into the future
Where everything is sentimental, where
Prognoses end up empty as hot air
And everyone's left puzzled and unsure.

Who knows what to think, or what to dream?
History! Throw a tantrum, or a crumb,
To prove the history of where we come from,
And me, and mine, will teach you how to scream.

VIII

Annamite traders in their little boats
Swarm round us, offering duck, fresh greens,

While we're still coaling. Stokers and marines
Lay off their tasks to barter while ships float

At anchor on the sooty bay, the French
Blaring through megaphones we must depart,
As Rozhestvensky drags his heels, *Descartes*
On the horizon, while I wield a wrench

On overworked machinery. Meanwhile,
On the *Oryol*, all hell has broken loose
In mutiny inspired by the bilge-juice
Served up as 'soup', and by the infantile

'Authoritarian' attitudes displayed
By officers who imitate the Admiral's
Pathetic blustering, his barks and bawls.
It's by the truths we do by which we're weighed

But Rozhestvensky needs to make his mark
On the 'ringleaders', and impose his lie
On any man who chooses to deny
His rights as judge, aristocrat, autarch.

And such. And such. And such as make men cry
Into their duty and their cups, steady
Before a wrathful Admiral. Ready, aye, ready!
Prepared to face the sailing samurai.

IX

And Rozhestvensky curses men and ships
With a vulgarity that's his self-portrait.
Thus fat old Folkerzham's the 'bag of shit'
While crude expletives issue from his lips

Whenever he has anything to say.
All bullies, though, are strong on scornful wit
And fear's the factor makes us laugh at it.
Ushakov's captain, one Miklikho-Maklay,

He calls a 'double-distilled idiot'
Being daft and drunken like his C-in-C,
While Bukhvostov, of *Alexander III*,
Ex-officer of Guards, invokes his spit

Before he pounces on his snobbishness –
And Rozhestvensky just exposes *his*
Flaws through his mouth's tyrannical assizes.
He takes a man's truth, then he makes it less,

Reducing him, 'cutting him down to size',
As he would say, when what he does is sever
All right to our respect, and our endeavour
For victory, which he seems to despise

As if we don't deserve his mediocre
Career and pedigree, risen rank by rank,
By 'connections', the magical gangplank
Of Empire. But he swears like a stoker

And that's why officers and men distrust him.
Rear-Admiral Enkvist, for example, slow
As he is, no intellectual, I saw throw
A tantrum and he openly cursed him

Who'd called him 'empty brain' – so one fool cursed
The fool who'd cursed *him*. And Captain Ber,
Commanding *Oslyabya*, a seducer,
A ladies' man (he thinks) discovered lust

Lampooned as 'lascivious carrion'
In a crack signal to the entire Fleet.
He answered Rozhestvensky: 'Hope *your* gleet
As painfully delivered as my own,

'You bastard.' *Woop*, *woop*! the sirens sang. *Woop*!
Then Rozhestvensky launched his mayhem of
Signals by flag and frantic heliograph –
'You syphilitic shit! You nincompoop!'

Serebrennikov, who skippers *Borodino* –
That happy ship – was flagged and flashed with flicks
Of insult for his youthful politics.
Suvorov's flags say he's a slave to *vino*

And 'nihilism', and, although it's true
That Captain keeps a cellar, it's a good one.
Friendly, hospitable, he suffers the sun
With elegantly chilled white wines, the dew

France reproduces year by vintage year.
While Serebrennikov worships such wine,
He keeps up, too, a cunning but benign
Populism. His men love him. There's no smear

In being the friend of the people. *If*
That's the case, then we should heave around
And disappoint our crazy, ironbound
Admiral, part sailor, part bumbailiff

To a dynasty, and his own self-regard.
Intent, though, on the war, and on 'his' battle –
But what we hear of that's mere tittle-tattle
Spread by gossips, big-mouths, sheer lies, canards,

Or nightmares turned come morning into rumour.
No, Rozhestvensky keeps us in the dark,
Commanding men and ships by spit and bark
As reason rots untouched by life or humour.

His principle is to humiliate
All and sundry, and give no thought to rank
For we're all liable to his un-thank
High-handedness, his brutal, triplicate,

Blunt, written memoranda or his yelled
Opprobrium, or eyes whacked black and blue
As if he doesn't know quite what to do
When someone disagrees, and so they're felled

By a blow to the head by a blow-hard
Bully. Ignatzius says: 'How much disgust
Must we endure before we earn his trust?
Do we want it? Rather his disregard

'Than his foul-mouthed attentions. He blacks eyes
Sooner than be civil. As for *discussion!* . . .
Well, his approach is well and truly Russian –
Sneer at the thought of it, and then despise

'Whoever's mischief dared even propose it.
I've tried to speak to him. What he intends
's his secret, or that's what he pretends.
The fact that he refuses to disclose it

'Could mean he 's *nothing* to disclose. His plan,
For all we know, is simply to steam north,
Coal-laden, on a prayer, for all we're worth,
Towards what's waiting for us off Japan.'

Then Rozhestvensky strolled into the wardroom.
'Conspiring, gentlemen?' he asked. 'Ah, drinking!
Now, some of you go in for too much *thinking* . . .
Leave that to *me*!' he yelled. To see him fume

Like that, although I know his mood too well –
We all do – chilled companionship with fear,
Because we know our Admiral 's sincere
In wishing all of us, and him, to Hell.

    X

Small, lanterned lights on sampans, row-boats, junks,
Exoticize the night. Their crewmen call
For business, but who's got the wherewithal
For trade these days? Over-promoted drunks

Lean on the rail and shout back lousy French
To lousy French in the French-policed bay.
I'd give my eye-teeth for snow and a sleigh
Tonight, for seen breath and the belled drench

Of something like a blizzard, and for you
Furred beside me, holding each other so
Around the shoulders as the horses throw
Manes and neighs. Not often, love, but we knew

Such white nights in the country, rugged and furred
Nights of the snowflaked kisses, nights of love
A million miles from noise-fraught *Suvorov*
Where dreams and memories get strangely blurred

By absences of touch and smell, your voice
Remembered but not heard, and your sweet kiss

Distant from me. Memory's pitiless . . .
And this, the profession of my *choice*!

XI

Where are your letters? – Lying in some morgue
The Admiralty dedicates to post
Then dedicates itself to getting lost
Or filed and pigeonholed in Petersburg.

I can't get used to absence. It hurts me.
Sore hours, days, weeks, months go by, and I cry
Silently, in verse, which can't dignify
Enough of what I feel – you, and the sea,

Or you and poetry, or you and me –
To put it simply. It's so lonely here.
Work and insult. Ship-noises like a sneer –
Monotonous autobiography!

It's shameful to admit to loneliness
But shameful not to if that's how you feel.
Such shame's so common here, and men conceal
Their miseries, the absence of kisses,

Pretending to a manly, naval pride,
Boasting of sweethearts, wives, or their freedom.
Wrapped in our solitudes, sheer tedium
Drives all of us into undignified

Habits – talking to oneself, or weeping
Over old letters, doing things like this
Act of self-preservation, this eye-witness
Account of self and soul, a word-keeping

Log and ledger, the inky stunt of it,
The slow scratch of the nib across the page
Enough to quieten me and soften rage
Under a buzzed lamp, composing my secret.

XII

Run-of-the-mill poetic types would give
Their eye-teeth for a subject such as this
Absence heading into danger. 'Loneliness',
They'd say, 'is bittersweet, and tastes of olive',

Or some such simile or metaphor,
When what it tastes of is your heart, *your* heart,
Sophie, and mine. Engineers don't know art.
That's our virtue. We make, and we adore

New things, which we invent. We understand
The future by instinct. And that's our gift.
That, too, is why I feel ashamed, adrift
In poetry, a curiously dry-land

Activity, it seems to me. Well, *should*
Poets in Russia object to me
Then all I can say is, 'You, go to sea!
Discover everything you've misunderstood

'Through being cooped up with eight hundred others
Whether on the high seas, or in anchorage,
Inflicted with the tedium of the age
And no two men here you could call your brothers.

'My verse lacks your sophistication, its
Command of style, and its modernity.

But then, I'm not of your fraternity,
Nor you of mine. I'm stuck with hulls, conduits,

'Electrics, armour, and machinery.
No escritoire from Muir and Mirrielees
Or plush chaise longue on which to take my ease
Before a swathe of chosen scenery!

'What I do, friends, is work, all day, all night
When there are tasks that only I can do
Or supervise dexterity and sinew,
And when I can 's the time when I can write.

'Exhausted privacy of page and pen
Helps keep me sane. I'm going to the dogs
In any case, by the shortcut of grog's
Bottled insanity, on the again

'And again principle, as if I need
To hurt my Muse before she'll come to me
Bearing my stint of rugged poetry,
My homely metre's passion, pain, and greed.

'How would you like a Mermaid Muse? Mine's draped
In seaweeds, skinned with scales and barnacles,
With eel-like hair, and eyes like miracles
For having stared too long at a seascaped

'Only world, waves, and calms, sea-creatures, life
In the wide wet, in the deep wet, the salt
Taste of her being, then the frightening jolt
When through scales, weeds and shells I see my wife

'Standing before me in my dream of my Muse.
A strange and large pain caused me to write this

Long screed of secret-jottered artifice.
I'm an *artificer*! And on a cruise

'To merry Hell, Japan, and smithereens . . .
My Muse goes with me, and if I survive –
She will! – then me, my work, and mine, will thrive;
If I don't, I'll be one of those has-beens

'Who never were! But then, I know physics,
Mechanics. I'm familiar with machines –
From latest gadgetry to blocked latrines! –
There's nothing in those lines that I can't fix.'

No, I don't ask you to relay my news
To better poet-peers at peace, at home,
Working at novelty, sucking the thumb.
Metamorphosed, please, please, remain my Muse!

XIII

On shore the forest fires paint scenes from Hell
In a night that brings the roars of elephants
On the breeze, like the cries of a great want
In the night, and the unfamiliar smell

Of burning wood, a very dry-land scent
To coal-burning sailors, coughing in coal-dust,
Cursing the circumstance or wanderlust
That brought them to this state of discontent.

Tomorrow we'll put out to sea, but where
We're going no one knows. Vladivostok?
The Admiral keeps his counsel. Mental block
Or secrecy? Does *he* know? Could he dare

Not risk a battle when we've steamed this far
Towards the chance of one, wherever it is
On ring-stained charts, in binoculars of his
Imagination where the proud memoir

Of his command and victory is published
To an imperial applause? We sail
To where our Admiral will win or fail.
Either we'll die, or else great things accomplished

May make us heroes. But I doubt that hope.
What can a fleet do when it can't supply
Decent provisions and can't answer 'Why?'
To shortages of food, post, clothes, and soap?

Enumerating these desiderata –
There could be more, much more, such as morale,
Skill, expertise, wisdom, and rationale –
Leaves me exhausted with the Fleet's errata

So that I feel light-headed, comic, grim
Before our dismal prospects, knowing that
If we should win I'll have to eat my hat,
And, worse, throw my hat high when cheering *him*.

XIV

England considers Japan her ally,
But that's because the English built their fleet
And trained their officers in the complete
Manual of naval what-to-do and why.

England sells coal to German merchants who
Sell Hamburg-Amerika coal, who sell

Coal to us. Everyone does very well
Out of these linked transactions, revenue

In large arithmetic distributed
Throughout the system of imperial power
Which asks no questions 'why?' or 'how?', or
If there 's something bad, corrupt or wretched

In money changing hands to keep a war
Profitable for some, lethal for others
Who play riskier roles while profit purrs
In many ledgers which the compradors

Death has appointed for this century
Examine in their offices' accounts,
Always for profit, not for loss, amounts
Such as would stagger Russia's soldiery

Except those officers who've purchased shares
In coals for us, and armaments against –
It's all available, not unlicensed
Or illegal. Men become millionaires

Trading in markets which can pull against
National interests. I've seen cruise by
Merchantmen of several nations, whose flags fly
Geographies of trade on the unfenced

World that we live in, but whose cargoes could,
Conceivably, be heading for Japan.
In all this dealing we're the also-ran,
Out-done and second rate. Ineptitude

Rules over us as if by a decree
Tsardom insists on, holding fast to its

Lunatic principles, its so-be-its
Shackled on us. Political ennui

Freezes us, even at this latitude.
We fester while we seek to justify
Indolent command's barked, aggressive lie.
Our loyalty's assured. A platitude

Guides us to destiny. What victory
Could ever be deserved by what we serve
And who? For where's the why of it? Our nerve,
Our fortitude, our courage, and our story,

Moan in the dungeon of obedience to
Style and stupidity as each deathtrap
Ship or boat salutes the million-saluted cap
To which we'll all prove silly, brave, and true.

XV

Kiss without lips. It's very hard to do!
You need to dream, and dream into a wind
From which all thoughts have been unfleshed and skinned
And on an open deck wide air blows through

Into the loneliness, into the truth.
But truth *is* lonely. Truth is solitude.
It's painful, bitter, beautiful, and good.
I kiss the air and stars with all my mouth.

Ignatzius caught me pouting at the stars.
'Old friend, our loneliness will meet its match
In battle, some day soon, and then we'll catch
Glory or shame, whatever's *rouge et noir*.

'So come to cards with me, my good old friend.
Drake played at bowls, but we shall play at cards!
Tomorrow we set sail for the dockyards
Of Hell or Vladivostok . . . Let it end.

'For there will be a stop to all these miles
Loneliness multiplies and sorrows keep
Treasured in restlessness, nightmared unsleep,
As if we love our loneliness's wiles

'Too much to be good for us. What it means
To be a sailor and to go to sea!
Fear not! We'll stand at wet Thermopylae
Together and discover the unseens

'Made visible at last! So, come and play.
I, too, miss love. I miss the Russian snow,
As you do, as you've said to me. I know,
Old friend, I know, I know. But each long day

'Grows shorter with digression. Each long night
Becomes less weary when a touch of fun
Brightens the boredom with that blaze of sun
Called laughter. If it' s all pretend delight,

'Then so be it as such. Escape, evasion,
Call it what you call it. I call it truth.'
I cried like a baby. Kiss without mouth.
Kiss without lips. And a big Asian

Moon hung over us. Sophie, I love you.
Tomorrow we'll steam out of Camranh Bay
And steer north to our Admiral's come-what-may,
His secret, charted spot, his rendezvous

With Togo and his British-built armada.
Over this perfumed sea I call to you
From the bay of elephants. I'm still true.
My cry is the cry of silent ardour.

PART EIGHT

I

Now that we're out at sea, and heading north,
It's time to say things straight and loud and clear –
Not that I haven't done before, my dear! –
But now it's louder, clearer, for what it' s worth.

The loneliness of men among men brings
An understanding of the finer things
In the lost rooms of love. Our seafaring
Feels overshadowed by domestic daring,

And rude men scribble thoughts of flowers
In the half-dark, and I remember you
In Samarkand in the Islamic blue
Under your parasol, our summer hours.

Work and profession stole our only time.
I let it happen, though. Obsessed with it.
Head over heels in love with a rivet!
Mad for machinery, grease, steel, and grime . . .

Now the ruffians lie down to sleep beside
Thieves, saints, aristocrats, and dream of youth.
'I looked into my self, and saw my truth.
I learned my foolishness; and then I died.'

II

Out of Camranh and now at Van Fong Bay
Instead of open sea . . . An engineer,

Kostenko, cut his foot. Only a year
Out of College (first prize!), but yesterday

I went to see him in the hospital-ship –
It's just the second time I've been aboard her.
We passed two sampans as we sailed towards her,
Hawking pumpkins and what looked like snipe

Or local long-beaked water-birds. No doubt
Officers still flush enough will buy them up
For Easter lunch – a snipe, and pumpkin soup . . .
That beats our galley's seaweed sauerkraut!

They don't get much mail there. But then, who does?
Nursing a cut Achilles tendon, he
Lingers among the coughs. An amputee
Grimaced – 'Sir, welcome to the slaughterhouse . . .'

Once there were six of us, trained engineers.
One's been sent home. Kostenko languishes.
Now we are four. Our strength diminishes.
And Rozhestvensky raves and interferes

With skills and work of which he's ignorant.
Well, Kostenko's safe. He's good and talented.
I'll miss his eagerness just when it's wanted,
Although, in battles, no one is important,

Or if they were those days are long since gone.
And empty, numbered beds, ward after ward,
Made me ask questions, but they went unanswered.
Names there turn into numbers, or Anon.

A Lenten lunch on *Oleg*, full of laughter . . .
One of the *Oleg*'s crew worked as a clown
Until disgrace or scandal brought him down.
At tricks and clowning he's a proper grafter

But it's a happy ship with more musicians
Than any other ship I've come across
In the entire Fleet – a different ethos,
One that owes nothing to our tired traditions.

When I got back, I found Ignatzius
Half-dressed in a deck-chair. 'It's nice like this,'
He said, though I stick to my prejudice –
Captains wear uniform, not 'something loose'.

Tropical greenery 's been brought aboard
For Easter, but the wardroom still looks wretched.
The bakers, though, have baked their usual bread
To look like Easter cakes. Multicoloured –

But where'd they get the paints? – baskets of eggs
Brought back the ritual Easters spent at home.
Was I alone in feeling overcome
By memory, unsteady on my legs

During the tented, suffocating service?
I stayed up late, slept in, and got up late –
'If any ship should need me, let it wait.'
Remiss of me, my semi-mischievous

Lethargy. Christ rose today, but I didn't,
At least not on time for the flag ceremony's
Uniformed piety, or the slow blaze
Of a South China Sea dawn, ancient,

Enormous. Later on, when *Suvorov*
Began to bore me, I found an excuse
To sail to *Borodino* where an obtuse,
Friendly command makes her my ladylove

Among our many ships. When I returned
To *Suvorov*, I sat on the forebridge
Inspecting the nocturnal anchorage
With Ignatzius. I've prickly heat. It burned

With a slow itch just below pain. Barefooted,
In his shirtsleeves, Ignatzius lounged and sipped,
A dandy who has let his standards slip,
Who doesn't notice when he's not saluted.

IV

Poor, stupid Golovko! He pilfered from
The wardroom sideboard's brandy, and got drunk –
His cushy billet, and my comfort, sunk
By his spontaneous gulp of odium.

He'll be punished, for sure. I'll have to seek
Another servant. I could speak to him.
Poor old Golovko whom I taught to swim!
His thirst was strong, and that's what made him weak,

As well as missing his wife and children.
Geography amazed him, terrorized
His dreams with distances that days disguised
With work and duty. He was wearing thin.

Now he's condemned to serve junior officers –
And that *is* punishment. I'll have a word

With one of them. Kindness can't be ordered,
Especially among these little sirs.

Forgiveness is forbidden by our code –
Still, I can try to help. What can I do?
If only old Golovko 'd asked me to,
I'd have slipped a bottle, and thought it owed.

Now I feel guilty that I didn't think
To ask Golovko if he'd like a drink.
'Sire', 'Your Honour' – not so much as a wink
At booze, nor did he ever smell of drink.

My servant wronged me, but I wronged my servant –
A Russian conundrum! But he's wrong,
I'm right. He's always wrong. And all along
We've known that what we think we have we haven't

In this life of demotion, punishment,
Offence and pain. I smoked a cigarette,
One of these French opium ones that whet
An appetite for sleep, diminishment,

A dwindled self, forgetfulness's friend.
Mildewed tobacco, Guadeloupe rum,
My candled partners in the Arts of Glum –
Just one more minute and the page is penned.

v

To satisfy the French, we put to sea,
Then we steamed back again into the bay.
This farce protects precious 'neutrality'
But gives me work to do. I jump like a flea

From one ship to another. Damaged hulls.
Blown valves. Poor old Golovko's been transferred.
He came to see me, weeping and absurd,
Pleading his honesty. I felt my pulse –

It was racing. The Admiral's been aboard
The battleship *Oryol*, whose mutinous crew
Threatened her officers. Give them their due,
Their officers are thoroughly deplored

Throughout the fleet, although the men are worse,
Recruited from jails, 'political lists',
And led by such incompetent reservists
Whose trick of leadership is to coerce

Men into discipline but not to duty.
But Rozhestvensky, he of the Old School,
Spoke for his officers, even that fool
Sidorov, who dances well, and loves beauty

In women, but who can't command a ship.
It's even worse on *Irtish*. She's awash
With boozed-up officers, led by a lush
Who lives to lean a bottle to his lip.

On *Gromky*, though, a boat came up to us
Oared by two Annamese, and with three boys
Beside them on the deck, little mikados,
Dressed to the nines, bowing and courteous,

With palms together (in prayer fashion).
They were for sale! From five to ten francs each!
That's cheaper than a pig. To buy a peach
From these boated traders costs a ration

Worth two weeks' cigarettes (with opium).
Ignatzius reprimanded me, and thought
I'd had it in my mind to buy the lot –
His little joke. Imagine, coming home

With three twelve-year-old Chinamen! And yet,
What poverty reduces them to sell
Children to strangers? It's a living Hell,
Or an amoral world of trade and profit,

Drives parents to surrender girls and boys
To fosterage, or servitude, or worse,
I thought, and felt a childless man's remorse.
Dusk-lighted sea was lilac, green, and turquoise.

VI

Delays. But Nebogatov's fleet arrived –
A sight out of the nineteenth century!
And old *Apraksin*, that floating mortuary,
In which I served five years ago, and skived

In days of peace. But still, we cheered, hurrah'd
These eminently sinkable old ships,
As Nebogatov's pinnace rode the dips
Towards the *Suvorov*, into the mad

Command of Rozhestvensky's unrevered
Strategy – no clear plan, only revenge
For Port Arthur, to vindicate, and plunge
Into the fires of wrath. But still, we cheered.

Another admiral – but I've lost count: how many? –
Might counsel him away from folly.

His charismatic, angry melancholy
Convinces others it's their destiny,

And ours, to follow him, as if he knows
Something we don't, a secret, or a dream,
Instead of puffed up with a self-esteem
He milks out of his mad mind and its shadows.

The Admirals shook hands. They kissed. Champagne!
It was like a regatta back at home
After imperial visits when we succumb
To self-flattery. It began to rain –

That gentle tap of rain-drops on tarpaulins.
On Admiral Nebogatov's epaulettes
Gold simmered in the polish of the wet.
'We needed that. We all needed a rinse,'

Ignatzius said to the *Apraksin*'s captain,
Holding his glass out to a waitered bottle.
The exchange of stories. The unstoppable
Eagerness. The rain on the tarpaulin

Above the capped heads, corks being popped
Amid reports of marvels, rumours, intrigue,
British duplicity, weathers, fatigue,
Unrest, and mutiny – hence three foretopped

Rifled marines keeping an eye on the decks.
The Admiral's speech was confident and brisk.
Its gist was simple – if you don't take a risk,
You won't win. Restrained, for him, his *lex*

Muscovia drained of expletives, pared down
For the occasion to pomposity,

Stern-faced and curseless bellicosity,
An Agamemnon of a country town

Let loose with an armada. Asian rain.
Can't he imagine carnage? Can't he smell
Modernity, its door that leads to Hell,
Its massiveness, its might, its blood, its pain?

We strolled to lunch. Through a Homeric mist
I saw the present in historic light –
Helmeted, sworded, tawny, a bit tight,
Whom wine and willing war-talk make immodest.

I overheard *Nicolai*'s captain say
To Nebogatov, 'What *are* his plans, sir?'
'None, as you ask. Just steam to the adventure.
He seems to see war as vindictive play,

'And serve the Tsar, and don't dare question me.
By God, the man can curse, I'll grant him that.
If he's worked out a plan, I'll eat my hat.
All I can say is, wait. We'll wait and see.'

VII

I quit the Admiral's table at a sprint –
Discourteous of me, but I'd heard
The mail 'd arrived! I longed for just one word
From you, then found my post *extravagant*

With parcels and letters. I didn't know
What to open first. Socks, sweets, handkerchiefs,
Soap, books, paper, eau-de-Cologne – its whiff's
Aromas civilized me, like a beau

On his birthday. The jam, though soldered well,
Leaked fruit; the cigarettes are smokable,
Though slightly spoiled. I couldn't get my fill
Of your letters, while those words you misspell –

We all do that, and I'm not criticizing –
Excite me, make you real again, for it's
Characteristics, quirks, those little habits
Identify us through an empathizing

Knowledge as large as love – a coffee-stain
On a page's corner, a fallen hair,
The distant scent of one who isn't there
Except in her handwriting, the profane

Details, iotas, what you did last night . . .
I couldn't read the newspapers you sent –
Too big, too undomestic, too intent,
Too wrong. I read you now by candlelight

Over and over. The insected fan
Whisks miniature lives in a buzzing cloud
That is my muffled, mouthless mind made loud
And multiple, the mind of lonely man

At his devotions, while a rat looks on
As if it' s sorry for me, and mosquitoes
Die in the candle-flame, in hot gallows –
Pzizz of wings and them, and then they're gone.

I sit among your letters and your presents
Dreading a call to some emergency
That means I have to dress and go away.
I'm so grateful. Thank you! My discontents

Rear over me like trash. There's work to do
Repairing this and that on *Suvorov*,
And that's for me to do, but I'm in love,
So let work wait while I re-re-read you

Once again, scanning your stains and your blots,
Your beautiful blots and stains, loveliness
In every nib-scratch of your ink's caress,
And the long kiss in your thoughts, and my thoughts.

Thank you. Thank you. To be remembered is
The best thing on this earth, and on its sea.
So many months, but you remember me!
I love you. Here's a heart-felt, paper kiss.

PART NINE

I

Many-pillared moonlight stalks our many ships
Tonight as we depart. Mere bibs and bobs . . .
Breakdowns. Repairs. The customary jobs.
The usual stuff, with salt caked on my lips.

Coal-dust, and rain makes sticky tar of it
Over the wet decks as it always does.
The sea shifts from its blacks to indigos
Of deep unstillness, its approximate

Profundity in the archive of charts.
Wave-driven rhetoric, a moonlit pen!
We're getting close. We think of 'why' and 'when'.
Answerless questions break twelve thousand hearts

While a pretence of merriment belays
Hot tears and trembles when men try to sleep
As soon as they're alone, and comradeship
Withers to nothing but the chat of days.

Some ships will leave us soon – Saigon, Shanghai –
And I'll get this aboard one. Others prefer
To wait for Vladivostok. I'm not so sure.
I'll put my faith in what I know 's deadeye

And almost certain, reckoned to a fact
As far as possible beyond the spell
Bewitching Lady Luck casts as farewell.
I'll say goodbye at the last minute, act

Without self-pity, as a man, without
Happy-go-lucky devil-may-care laughter
Placing all its chance in a hereafter.
A half-drunk priest, with boys, goes round – God's tout –

Decks, cabins, berths, bestowing blessings on
Unblessable bluejackets, even on me
Whose God 's become the meaning of the sea
Rising out of the storms or calms of dawn.

And now we coal again. The ships are rolling
In the muscular swell. It's very hot.
Those heaving coal work in a coffee pot,
The way it's always been when we've been coaling

On this authoritative, epic voyage.
It will be different soon. It will grow cold.
And men and boys will shiver and grow old,
Or older when the weather's subterfuge

Slips wisdom to them, knowledge of a north
That they've forgotten in their months at sea
Under St Andrew's flag of the unfree
On the hot waters of tropical unmirth.

II

God knows how many lines I've written down.
But now I come to think of it, I write
Always remembering the day, at night,
By lantern or by candlelight, alone

And blowing smoke at flies while other men
Snore, cough, or stagger through their dreams of home.

Involuntarily, the sleepers comb
Memory where the sanity of then

Resolves the madness of the present tense.
And I do too. And yet I write of now
In this half-suffocated noise, and plough
A nib across the paper of white silence.

I'm told Formosa isn't far away,
'The floral island', said to be exquisite.
I told Ignatzius I'd like to visit it.
'Don't worry, Flag. Perhaps some other day,

'On the long cruise home from Vladivostok.'
Not even he suspects I'm writing this
Nocturnal diary. I blow my kiss
Into the alphabet and hear the clock

Keep time and rhythm like a metronome
Although I write more to my own heartbeat
Than artificial measures. Poetic 'feet'
Shod in the heart's smithy for life, love and home! . . .

Clippety-clop. I'm riding boyhood's pony
Once again, with my father beside me
And years before I'd ever seen the sea
Or knew that I was born to tyranny

And naval architecture, born to learn
Habits and prejudices of my caste
And born to serve the Tsar before the mast,
Born to unlearn what I was born to learn.

Only Golovko knows. But he can read.
The only man who's peeped into my papers

Made nothing of them, just – 'These, sire, are yours.'
But you know, Sophie. Each obsessive screed

Goes in the post to you, and soon we'll shed
Unnecessary vessels to Shanghai.
I've things to write by then, before I die,
Or live, but when I do, let them be read

By Mr Censor (who hates verse), by you,
Or anyone who shows an interest
In lines from this pen-crippled naval wrist.
Crude as they are, they're nothing if not true.

III

Sea-burials in the life-laden sunlight
Four times today. Saddened, all I could do
Was watch through glasses as I wondered who.
And, if I knew them, then, how could I write

A suitable remembrance without shame
Coming between me and their cut-short lives?
There's something secret of us that survives.
Each weighted box sank with a dead man's name

After a short-lived splash and a few strains
From small bands as the massive fleet steamed on
Towards an X to which its Admiral 's drawn
By dreams or destiny or fuddled brains.

Ungardenable wilderness, all salt
And covert flesh, teeth, stings, its tilting deeps
A no-place where a monstrous nothing sleeps
In the Darwinian depths, almost-occult,

Ocean is dangerous, most beautiful
In any of its moods. For who could choose
Between its blue calm and its swelling bruise
Before the storm, its wet and pitching thrill?

That boy in Tashkent, little did he know
What would his fate be when his mother's promise
To take him to the sea turned out like this.
She kept her promises of sea and snow

But it was sea I loved, its alien
Remoteness and its trick of distances
Pulling against all five active senses
And the skin feels lively in the warm rain.

IV

We call it contraband, they call it trade
In the neutral steamers that our cruisers stop
And search on the high seas, each floating shop
A treasure trove – gun-cotton, marmalade,

Explosives, soap, a large array of wines,
Rifles, machine-guns, shells, horses(!), and steel,
Nosebags, jute sacks, copper, flour, oatmeal,
Tinned foods and milk, holds packed with railway lines . . .

One's destinations were found out to be
First Yokohama, then Vladivostok.
They sell to both sides and they laugh and mock
At those who gag on trade and irony.

Jemchug signalled that she'd seen a balloon
Above her. Other ships reported it

As snake-shaped, but from where I sit
It was a Chinese kite crossing the moon

Escaped from the Formosan coast today
On a snapped string, where a grandfather stood
On a windy beach with his children's brood
In the sensation of a flyaway

Free'd kite, the pathos of the old and young –
But I'm imagining! Is it a sign
That life is wrong with me, that I imagine,
Preferring memories, their under-sung

Lyrical drift, an inexact recall
Of half a tune, a broken line, a face
But not a name, a name but not the face?
Ah, where I've been! Tangier and Senegal,

Gabon! . . . No sight, though, of the Japanese
Who must be waiting for us up ahead,
Fresh, fast, contented, resolute, well fed,
Manning the armoured pride of Tyne and Tees.

It's out of date, the atlas that I used
At school, but it's the one I read. My eyes
Still take me to pagodas, foreign skies
And desert islands where my boyhood cruised

In life's longed-for lagoons, as if I've wished
Always for distance and for solitude.
No matter how I love you, I elude
You and myself, and crave to be diminished.

I can't help it. It is the fact of me.
My mother took me to the snow. I loved

Being overcoated, mufflered, and gloved.
And then my mother took me to the sea.

V

I'm now prepared for battle, having stowed
All my belongings in my cabin trunk –
My souvenirs from where I've been, much junk
From Africa, dead clothes, and the yellowed

Sheets of your letters to me, photographs
Of you, and this in my battered jotter
Well-wrapped in oilskins to protect from water
In case we're sunk. Good old Ignatzius laughs

At my precautions, for I've told him that
I've passed my night-watch writing verse to you.
I had to tell him. But he said he *knew*.
'I know. I've always known. Golovko spat,

'Then rubbed his spit into the quarterdeck
Before he cleared his throat, and told me he
Was very worried for you, writing poetry
All night. He thought you were mad, or a wreck,

'Or cracking up. He can read, and he knew
That what he watched you writing was a poem.
That's Old Russia for you! Blow me if I'm
Indifferent to my officers and crew,

'But old Golovko sobered me, because
Although he could read it, and he could see
That what you'd written down was poetry,
He *didn't* read it, but just saw what it was.

'I've far too much to do today, or else
I'd offer you a connoisseur's critique.
My God, an engineer! Well, you've a cheek . . .
I'll read it later, Vladivostok, Hell's

'Library, or wherever we fetch up.'
Dear friend, Ignatzius! Yes, I'll let him read
My amateur epistles' scribbled screed
On absence, water, love, and the far Europe

Which, I'm convinced, will suffer this century
As no other. Suffering 's relative –
Of course it is. I wish I'd time to live
And learn more, but I'm stuck in penury

As far as time's concerned. Our Admiral's
Hell-bent on battle in the narrow straits
Between Korea and Japan. He hates
Japan, the Japanese, and now he drills

His Staff in loathing for our enemy.
He shouts and barks at us – '*You must despise
Our dwarfy foe, those men with little eyes!*'
He's set our course for death and infamy.

I'll have to hurry. Our unarmed transports
Will leave us soon for Shanghai, and with mail
If I can finish this before they sail
To booze and safety and the sexual sports

For which the city's famous. Not for me!
My uniform's been pressed, so if I die
I'll be well dressed, gold cufflinks, black bow-tie,
Wing collar, dressed to meet the horrid sea.

Flag-Engineer Eugène Sigismondovitch Politovsky was born in Tashkent in 1875 and perished on the flagship *Suvorov* during the battle of Tsushima in May 1905. No eye-witness account of his death has come to light, but it seems likely to have occurred early in the battle. Admiral Rozhestvensky survived, although badly wounded. He was treated in captivity and nursed back to health by the Japanese. Admiral Togo, the Japanese commander, seems to have respected his enemy, but he could also have been grateful for his errors of judgement. On the other hand, in the opening minutes of the battle the fall of shot from the Russian fleet was more accurate than that of the Japanese, causing around 500 casualties, and obliging some Japanese vessels to fall out of the line. Shortly after, though, 'turning the T' of the formations involved, the Japanese fleet was able to bring almost all its fire-power to bear on the Russian flagship. Given that Politovsky was one of the few qualified 'engineer-constructors' aboard the Russian fleet, and the only one on *Suvorov*, he would have been engaged on repair work and exposed to the heaviest of the enemy fire, whether above- or below-decks.

Known as 'the Trafalgar of the East', Tsushima is recorded by historians as the biggest naval gun-battle in history, and a more decisive sea-battle than Trafalgar itself. In Japanese, Tsushima means 'the Donkey's Ears', a description of the appearance of the twin peaks of the islands near which the battle was fought.

I'm aware of Sir Henry Newbolt's *The Year of Trafalgar*, and his *Poems of Trafalgar*, and can assure readers that I have no inclination to join his company. What I find striking, though, is the comparison of politics and technology in the hundred years between Nelson's victory and Admiral Togo's.

Published eye-witness accounts of the battle include one by Captain Vladimir Semenov, *The Battle of Tsu-Shima* (London, John Murray, 1906). Semenov was aboard the flagship in the capacity of an observer, and was taken off in the company of his Admiral and several other officers of the Staff. At the end of his book he quotes a Japanese description of the last moments of the *Suvorov*:

In the dusk, when our cruisers were driving the enemy northwards, they came upon the Suvorov *alone, at some distance from the fight, heeling over badly and enveloped in flames and smoke. The division (Captain-Lieutenant Fudzimoto) of torpedo-boats, which was with our cruisers, was at once sent to attack her. Although much burned and still on fire – although she had been subjected to so many attacks, having been fired at by all the fleet (in the full sense of the word) – although she had only one serviceable gun – she still opened fire, showing her determination to defend herself to the last moment of her existence – so long, in fact, as she remained above water. At length, at about 7 p.m., after our torpedo-boats had twice attacked her, she went to the bottom.*

By then, almost all of *Suvorov*'s crew must have been dead or incapacitated. The Japanese report, like many others, doesn't suggest cowardice. Indeed, it would seem that the Russian defeat, and the Japanese victory, were chiefly the result of the excessively long and exhausting voyage from the Baltic to the Straits of Korea, and then of Admiral Rozhestvensky's personality and weaknesses as a commander, bad luck, and the acumen and skill of Admiral Togo, especially his patience in waiting for his enemy to come to him.

A. Novikov-Priboi's *Tsushima: Grave of a Floating City* (English translation, 1937) has been described as a novel. If it is such it is because it contains dialogue. Its author served on the battleship *Oryol*, notorious, or celebrated, in the Russian fleet for its many dissidents and revolutionaries. Appearing during the Stalinist, Soviet period, and written by an adherent, as well as a survivor of the battle and of Japanese captivity, it contains much eye-witness vigour as well as a certain ideological relish. More recently, Richard Hough's *The Fleet That Had to Die* (1958) provides a readable, journalistic and under-referenced account of the voyage and the battle.

I didn't describe the battle for the simple reason that my narrator didn't survive it and therefore couldn't write home to his wife about what had befallen him. If this is thought to be a pity then no one feels it more sorely than I do. At times I felt that I had become my narrator, and I didn't much care for the experience. Having begun the poem in 1983 at the request of the Ferens Art Gallery, which mounted an exhibition on the Dogger Bank Incident (as history now knows it), I went slightly beyond the fundless commission of its then Director, John Bradshaw, and wrote Part One of the poem at more length in response to a loan of Politovsky's posthumous *From Libau to Tsushima* made by Brian Lewis, the artist whose work illustrated the exhibition. Called 'The Day the Russian Imperial Fleet Fired on the Hull Trawlermen', the exhibition ran from 9 April to 8 May in 1983 and was one of a series on the theme of 'A People's History of Yorkshire'. At the time, it was meat and drink to me, as some of my old drinking companions in The Avenues pub were former trawlermen, and the Dogger Bank Incident was an intimate part of Hull lore. My poem was published shortly after in the now-defunct magazine *Encounter*. It lay dormant for at least two or three years, until I found myself adding bits to it. In the summer of 1997 I found myself returning to it 'full time' (as it were, although with a demanding day-job this meant writing at night in the same way as Politovsky). Partly this was due to an abhorrence of leaving a piece of work unfinished. Also, I felt an instinctive need to write a poem about the twentieth century.

Some readers may object to my having made Politovsky a poet, even a secret one, when he never was. I admit to an anxiety here.

But then I have admitted to the sources of my fiction, which many writers don't. Also, I've departed from his published letters only when I've felt it could be justified by the non-rules of fiction and the even less intransigent 'rules' (but they don't exist) of poetry (or of its attempt). What rules I've followed are those of ethics, and they do exist, and of imagination, which don't exist but which any writer responsible to time and people hopes to serve.

DOUGLAS DUNN
DAIRSIE, 19 AUGUST 1999